The Underground Poetry Metro
Transportation System for Souls

Tony Hoagland

The Underground Poetry
Metro Transportation System
for Souls

ESSAYS ON THE CULTURAL LIFE
OF POETRY

UNIVERSITY OF MICHIGAN PRESS

Ann Arbor

Published in the United States of America by the
University of Michigan Press
Printed and bound by CPI Group (UK) Ltd, Croydon, CR0 4YY

A CIP catalog record for this book is available from the British Library.

First published October 2019

Library of Congress Cataloging-in-Publication Data

Names: Hoagland, Tony, author.
Title: The underground poetry metro transportation system for souls : essays
    on the cultural life of poetry / Tony Hoagland.
Other titles: Cultural life of poetry
Description: Ann Arbor : University of Michigan Press, 2019. | Series: Poets on
    poetry
Identifiers: LCCN 2019033188 (print) | LCCN 2019033189 (ebook) | ISBN
    9780472037575 (paperback) | ISBN 9780472126163 (ebook)
Subjects: LCSH: Poetry—History and criticism. | Poetry—Themes, motives. |
    Poetry—Appreciation. | Poetry—Influence. | Poetry.
Classification: LCC PS3558.O3355 A6 2019 (print) | LCC PS3558.O3355
    (ebook) | DDC 808.1—dc23
LC record available at https://lccn.loc.gov/2019033188
LC ebook record available at https://lccn.loc.gov/2019033189

Acknowledgments

Some essays in this volume were previously published elsewhere:

The AWP Writer's Chronicle: "Ceremony and Discrimination: Two Muscles of Poetry," 2017; "What These Ithakas Mean: Some Thoughts about Metaphor and Questing," 2018; "'I Live My Life in Growing Orbits': Robert Bly as Role Model," 2017; "The Poet as Wounded Citizen," 2018; "Poetry, the Dangers of Realism and the Revisionist Power of Fantasy," 2019

American Poetry Review: "'What You See Is Nothing Compared to the Root': Images of the Psyche in the Poem," 2018; "'I Seem to Be at a Great Feast': The War Poems of Guillaume Apollinaire," 2014; "Going Crosstown: Four Poems about Race by White Poets," 2016; "No Laughing Matter: Race, Poetry, and Humor," 2015

The Auden Journal: "'Who Wished to Improve Us a Little by Living': Remembering Auden's Influence"

Humor: International Journal of Humor Research: "Cast Swine before Pearls: Comedy, Shamanic Rage, and Poetry," 2009

Gulf Coast: "Mass Culture and the American Poet: The Poem as Vaccination"; "Greatness Is All Around Us," 2019

New Ohio Review: "The Pursuit of Ignorance: The Challenging Figuration of Not Knowing"; "The Power of Coldness"; "The Wild Life of Metaphor: Prehensile, Triangulating, Insubordinate," 2018

Contents

Digital materials related to this title can be found on the
Fulcrum platform via the following citable URL:
https://doi.org/10.3998/mpub.11375608

"What You See Is Nothing Compared to the Root"

Images of Psyche in the Poem

"The poets and philosophers before me," said Freud, "discovered the unconscious. . . . What I discovered was the scientific method by which the unconscious could be studied." He and his analytical brethren drew their descriptions of how the psyche works from two sources: their own case studies, and from poetry and literature. In those narratives and poems, they sought to identify the myths, patterns, compulsions, and desires which structure human nature and narrate the human condition. Thus Hamlet and Oedipus; Richard III, and the inferiority complex.

What Freud perhaps did not guess was that psychoanalysis itself would, in the twentieth century, stamp *its* narratives onto contemporary literature; that poets and fiction writers would adopt, imitate, and reproduce the insights of psychoanalysts in the making of their fictions. Given the tools and the vernacular of psychology, they would read experience differently. Twentieth-century writers would construe their stories in the idiom of psychoanalysis, as much as the other way around.

Psychoanalysis made Sylvia Plath possible, and John Berryman, and Anne Sexton. From W. H. Auden to Ernest Hemingway, from Alfred Hitchcock to Lillian Hellman, psychoanalysis informed how we saw things, what we thought about, and how we sounded when we talked. Its narratives and its jargon provided an idiom that pervaded films, novels and poetry for sixty or seventy years.

Here, for example, are two passages from well-known poems that could not, and would never have been written without psychoanalytic thought and jargon in the community water supply:

Whoever despises the clitoris despises the penis
Whoever despises the penis despises the cunt
Whoever despises the cunt despises the life of the child.
Resurrection music,   silence,   and surf.
　　　　　—Muriel Rukeyser, "The Speed of Darkness"

The Greeks are sitting on the beach
wondering what to do when the war ends . . .

Thinking things over in the hot sun, pleased
by a new strength in their forearms, which seem
more golden than they did at home, some
begin to miss their families a little,
to miss their wives, to want to see
if the war has aged them. And a few grow
slightly uneasy: what if war
is just a male version of dressing up,
a game devised to avoid
profound spiritual questions?
　　　　　—Louise Glück, "Parable of the Hostages"

Contemporary theoreticians have encouraged us to suspect all ideologies, to see them as a kind of disease which human beings are prey to, as intellectual viruses that fog the mind and promote mass hysteria, as embedded systems which maintain social inequities. This position may seem true enough if one thinks only of the Spanish Inquisition, or Nazism, or the Cold War, but that's not the whole story. Systems of belief—psychoanalysis being one of many—don't just harness and bully culture; they lend it shape and empower it; they lend it a vocabulary for the world; they extend its reach and strengthen its grasp.

As mythology once structured the Greek imagination, as Christianity adopted its three-tiered system (heaven-earth-hell), psychoanalysis gave artists of all kinds a framework that encompassed the known and the unknown, the civilized and the savage, the personal past and the challenging present. Psychoanalysis provided a way of accounting for human nature and culture required by the modern individual to situate herself in a story. Psychoanalysis offered a torch (or a flashlight) that could be used to look into the dark of dreams and neurosis, and to extend the light of insight.

In forties and fifties America, it was psychoanalytic vocabulary—*neurosis, Oedipus complex, boundary issues, penis envy, sibling rivalry, inferiority complex, narcissistic*—that became our common intellectual currency. On TV shows like the Jack Parr show, in comedy routines like those of Bob Newhart and Woody Allen, in child rearing manuals (Dr. Spock), psychoanalysis—both mocked and taken seriously—fully infiltrated modern middlebrow culture. Deprived of our confidence in a supreme deity, the average citizen-self had become more frail and naked, more existentially vulnerable in the universe. On the other hand, thanks to the new cosmos of psychology, the self was granted a sort of capaciousness; it could dream, and free-associate, and talk bitterly about its parents. A person was itself a sort of colony of contradictory instincts and ideas, a place itself mysterious and worthy of exploration.

1. Working It Out

If you want to see the impact of psychology upon our poetry, examples abound. "The Anxiety," by Michael Dennis Browne provides a textbook representation, in poetic form, of the therapeutic process:

> I don't expect the anxiety to go away
>   but I want the anxiety to know
> its place in the scheme of things
>   of which I seem to consist.
> I want the anxiety to be
>   not an attention-getter or star
> but faceless, like a butler bearing trays,
>   whose old hand has turned down my bed,
> who knows when to take his leave,
>   the one I could even grow to pity,
> this trembling retainer I keep on,
>   as my father before me,
> out of some kind of long-standing
>   loyalty to the anxiety family,

whose fortunes have been bound up
  with ours for so long.

"The Anxiety" offers a lucid, almost letter-perfect version of the therapeutic process. It showcases a speaker confronting and patiently working through a psychological affliction towards a better accommodation. This is what Freud called "the talking cure" in action.

Browne's poem could not have been written without the theories of Sigmund Freud and the existence of the psychoanalytic framework and vocabulary. The analytic term *anxiety* was needed to provide the speaker with the necessary degree of separation from his own subjective condition to be able to have a dialogue with it. Because the speaker is conceptually comfortable with the idea that the psyche is compartmentalized and split—those parts can enter into negotiation with each other.

The speaker of Browne's poem seems like a person who has already done a certain amount of therapeutic work. After all, he is engaged in a process of dialogue with a part of his internal unconscious constituency: anxiety. From a psychoanalytic perspective, moreover, the requests of this spokesperson for the ego are quite reasonable: he has a desire for a more comfortable existence, one in which a better balance is achieved between function and dysfunction. He wants anxiety "to know / its place in the scheme of things." Such a proportionate sense of the relative nature of happiness is one benchmark of Freud's so-called "well-adjusted" human being.

And indeed, at the end of the poem, the speaker's psyche *is* convincingly reorganized; his parts seem reconciled with each other.

How is this breakthrough in "The Anxiety" achieved? In part, as mentioned, it is facilitated through the enterprise of dialectical conversation. The other poetically-interesting ingredient is the active agency of associative imagination in the poem. It is when the poem's speaker personifies his anxiety as a kind of *servant* or *comforter*—only then can he find an attitude of compassion toward this former adversary. By the end of the poem, the speaker has accepted the anxiety as a kind of companion, with whom he *must*, with whom he has *always* cohabited.

Such a poem is not just a product of psychological culture, it is a model of the mysterious psyche of language in action. In the complex textures of the poem, we see upwelling energies and strata, the collaborating energies of conscious and unconscious resources. If the conscious self brings the resources of rationality, choice, discernment and will, then the unconscious brings to the table imagination and play, song and theatre.

On a sheerly linguistic level, this process becomes visible in "The Anxiety" in a kind of quickening or turbulence that begins around line eight. Once the personification of the butler has been introduced, the second half of the poem is riddled with puns, double entendres, and ambiguities: a "retainer," for example, is something that holds one back, as well as a servant; that the figure is "long-standing" suggests the way in which a butler is stereotypically seen as perpetually standing at attention; that the "fortunes" (meaning both money and fate) of the two characters in the poem are "tied-up" suggests that they have held each other in a state of captivity. These sonic and punning elements are evidence of the simmering, ingenious participation of the deep imagination in the making of the poem.

2. Entanglement

"The Anxiety" is a monologue with a therapeutic happy ending: one in which the parts of the psyche, formerly at odds, learn to cooperate, converse, and live harmoniously together.

But the layers of the self are not usually so easily disentangled. Poems often testify to and embody entanglement as well. And there is something both revelatory and cathartic about seeing even the most insoluble or toxic conundrums of selfhood vividly represented and brought to crisis. It can be consoling and clarifying to see such images of the entangled self. In contrast to Michael Dennis Browne's patient, reasonable poem, Robert Creeley's poem "Mother's Voice" enacts a less detached psychological state of enmeshment in a more dire and physical way.

In these few years
since her death I hear

mother's voice say
under my own, I won't

want any more of that.
My cheekbones resonate
with her emphasis. Nothing
of not wanting only

but the distance there from
common fact of others
frightens me. I look out
at all this demanding world

and try to put it quietly back,
from me, say, thank you,
I've already had some
though I haven't

and would like to
but I've said no, she has,
it's not my voice anymore.
It's higher as hers was

and accommodates too simply
its frustrations when
I at least think I want more
and must have it.

Creeley's poem begins in a narrative and level-headed mode, but in line seven the voice begins to grow strange, incoherent, and abstract. The distortion of syntax and grammar of the poem actively mirrors the internal confusion of the speaker's self. The sentences themselves embody the deformity and adhesions of the speaker to the mother, like an egg stuck to the wall of the ovary. This internal theatre of conflicting voices is recognizable, to some degree, to even the most normal among us, but Creeley's representation of this dreadful confusion is brilliant. The poem displays a predicament of hell, an underworld of incomplete separation which itself radically estranges the speaker from the "common fact of others."

Like the earlier poem by Michael Dennis Browne, Creeley's poem is highly informed by the psychoanalytic blueprint of self-development. Despite the poem's bleak scenario, we can see the speaker's self working to gain a critical distance on the limits of this self-denying legacy: it "accommodates too simply / its frustrations," the speaker reasons, in his conscious rebellion against the frozen past. The struggle of language itself manifests a heroic effort towards autonomy. Even inside the prison, there is the glimmer of hope for change.

3. Archetype

Like Creeley's poem, Louise Glück's poem "Mock Orange" is about being <u>stuck</u>, jammed deep inside the human predicament. Like a cramped muscle, the psyche in "Mock Orange" clenches its own trauma like a fist. "Mock Orange" is gripping in its raw intensity and force.

Yet there is an important categorical difference between the two performances. Creeley's poem—in its opening at least—is clearly channeled through the paradigm of psychological method—it is, we could say, underwritten by the insights of therapy. ("In these few years / since her death I hear / mother's voice say under my own") By contrast, in reading or listening to Glück's "Mock Orange," we are transported into the realm of myth and archetype.

It is not the moon, I tell you.
It is these flowers
lighting the yard.

I hate them.
I hate them as I hate sex,
the man's mouth
sealing my mouth, the man's
paralyzing body—

and the cry that always escapes,
the low, humiliating
premise of union—

In my mind tonight
I hear the question and pursuing answer
fused in one sound
that mounts and mounts and then
is split into the old selves,
the tired antagonisms. Do you see?
We were made fools of.
And the scent of mock orange
drifts through the window.

How can I rest?
How can I be content
while there is still
that odor in the world?

This distinction between the personal and the archetypal voice is a significant one, poetically and psychically. The poetics of personal psychology are *local* and autobiographical; such a poem seeks insight and resolution in the voice of a struggling and good-willed individual. The poetic voice often emanates an urgent intimacy. The improvement of the speaker's circumstances is a real possibility.

The high-pitched monologue of the archetype is another story; such a monologue embodies an eternal conundrum, a universally-recurring, permanent locus of human consciousness—the proud, unforgiving Creon, the abandoned and fatalistic Dido, the eternally grieving mother pieta. When we read "Mock Orange," we are listening to an old story, told by one of those selves from the deep interior of the collective consciousness. The lyric, ferocious complaint is a perpetual configuration of consciousness and of human affairs; it will always be so, and the particular players are merely the temporary, temporal mouthpieces for the gods, demons, and goddesses present.

"Mock Orange" is the complaint of one who has fallen from erotic grace, exiled from the realms of true pleasure and union. At the core of the poem is a wound, a complaint, and a renunciation. Though Glück assigns the speech to no particular mythic character (as she does elsewhere in her poetry), it is easy to imagine the speaker as one of the angry virgin goddesses who pledges never to be captured and deflowered; or perhaps one of the many mythological figures—usually female—who have been loved and then abandoned by a god.

Though the poem's acidic complaint about sex is unforgettable—"I hate them. / I hate them as I hate sex, / the man's mouth / sealing my mouth"—what the speaker truly hates is not sex, but the promise, the premise, of an achievable *oneness*, a longing which is always disappointed. Here is the tragic truth of the archetype: the selves that attempt union always fall back into their condition of separateness. The failure of union is inevitable and irresolvable. Glück's poem is the expressed outrage of that condition of existential partialness.

In that sense, the plot of "Mock Orange" is practically the opposite of the Michael Browne poem, which illustrates a successful, if modest, psychological union and integration. A New Age therapist, encountering Glück's speaker as a client, would wrinkle his brow sympathetically and say, "But don't you see? You must find the eternal lover inside *yourself*."

But Glück's poem embodies a cosmic dilemma, and will not soften its existential extremity. Because the poem is archetypal in orientation, we can glimpse the specter of other myths floating around the perimeter of this one—the exile from Eden into shame and incompleteness; Eurydice in the underworld after slipping from the grasp of Orpheus; Psyche sent away by Cupid. No flower will ever be aromatic again; no food will ever again taste good.

But remember, poems are made great by their imaginative resources, not their conceptual strengths. One brilliant aspect of Glück's poetic craft is its figurative genius—the way in which the speaker turns abstractions into metaphors that configure the theme of mating and romance. In stanza four, for example, she says "in my mind tonight / I hear the question and pursuing answer," providing an analogy for both carnal and intellectual desire. Then, when the answer catches the question (an interesting reversal), they "fuse" into "one sound," that first "mounts and mounts"—again the sexual analogy—then "is split into the old selves / the tired antagonisms." It is not just the futility of passion that is being lamented by the speaker, it is the uselessness of intellect as well. We will never be a finished thought, we will never be more than a temporary answer, nor will we ever be more than temporarily whole.

In "Mock Orange," the hatred of isolate discreteness is projected onto sex—the world of men and women and copulation—and that hatred of sex is transferred or projected into the smell of nighttime flowers. The speaker is a barren ghost wandering restlessly in a sensuous world, a mythological figure tormented by some memory of union which eludes her. Her response is to accuse the world of a cosmic breach of faith. And, fair enough. This too is a true image of the process of the psyche, which keeps transforming, struggling for an achievement it only falls away from.

4. Alternative Models of Psyche

Creeley's and Glück's poems both provide images for—and the poems themselves create—the sensation of being trapped. Specifically, we might even say, the poems express the feeling of being trapped in *bodies*. Each of these poems encloses the speaker's self to a point of suffocation, then intensifies the crisis to a point at which a breakthrough can occur. "How can I be content [?]" asks Glück's speaker, caught in herself forever like a maiden trapped in stone. "But I've said no, she has, / it's not my voice anymore," says Creeley's afflicted speaker. Alienated, separate, and needy: the image is an old one. The underlying request— *Help me*—is the very foundation of psychology.

Just as we say that metaphorical systems empower, they can also ensnare. Ask any Catholic. How can we find an image then, or a system, that can reverse, unlock, transform, or liberate us from the model of the world, or of the psyche, that we have unconsciously inherited? For it is plentifully evident that the parameters of psychoanalysis have ensnared numerous seekers over the years—those whose analysis never ends, those who become addicted to their trauma, those for whom an esoteric vocabulary has become a substitute for life.

The answer might reside in working with the images with which we describe our world. Psyche *is* image, says Carl Jung. Images are pre-rational, and carry information from the other worlds into this one—ergo mythology and folklore. Images, and the psychic possibilities they represent, can teach us in ways that

10

bypass and circumvent the analytical mind. Imagination can discover the unimaginable.

The Swedish poet Tomas Tranströmer, a child psychologist by profession, often displays in his poems an awareness which incorporates yet also enlarges the parameters of psychology. Tranströmer writes poems that frame consciousness in a less boundaried way than the sheerly psychological. His imagistic vocabulary even illuminates the assumptions and limitations of the older system.

One novel aspect of Tranströmer's "analytics" is that they do not depict the world as exclusively human-centered. In Tranströmer's poems, the human is coexistent with, but not essentially separate from or superior to, the natural world. The consequences of such expansiveness are evident in his poem "A Few Moments" translated by Robert Bly:

> The dwarf pine on marsh grounds holds its head up: a dark
> rag.
> But what you see is nothing compared to the roots,
> the widening, secretly groping, deathless or half-
> deathless root system.
>
> I you she he also put roots out.
> Outside our common will.
> Outside the City.
>
> Rain drifts from the summer sky that's pale as milk.
> It is as if my five senses were hooked up to some other
> creature
> that moves with the same stubborn flow
> as the runners in white circling the track as the night comes
> misting in.

In Tranströmer's poem, Nature itself models the true connectedness of things better than human institutional wisdom. The root system of the self, to use the poem's analogy, is larger than the spread-out branches of the tree visible above ground. The boundaries of this world are not the penitentiary walls of an isolated human individual; they are permeable, contiguous, and in communication with their surroundings, like the dwarf pine.

Here, awareness flows out of the individual speaker into the surrounding world. Here, physical energy is spiritual energy, and it is in circulation: "I you she he also put roots out." In Freudian analysis, the unconscious contains disturbing and repressed elements. In Tranströmer's more Jungian-influenced vision, the unconscious is simply the water in which we all swim, the air we breathe, the earth upon whose surface we walk. "Outside the city" there is more of us and we are alive. Such an image surprisingly heartens us.

The intentional plainness of the Tranströmer poem, and the opaque, somewhat surreal image at its conclusion, have their own meanings. The covert import of such plain language is that "No fancy linguistic fluency nor style will easily get us out of our predicament." The human psyche contains some bleak realities, Tranströmer acknowledges, as well as graceful, natural ones. The idea of being in control, of achieving some permanent state of harmony or safety is a pipe dream. We must not pretend to be more evolved than we are. To have a split consciousness, a split being, to be "hooked up to some other creature," is the human condition, and to deny that is folly. As the half-formed images in the last lines of "A Few Moments" suggest, we are incomplete and "secretly groping." But we are also larger than we might think.

The final stanza of Tranströmer's "A Few Moments" has a rough, unfinished, resistant quality that I think is intentional. As a late twentieth-century European who had witnessed the rise and dissolution of ideological systems aplenty, Tranströmer often reiterates this point about incompleteness. In another poem, "Romanesque Arches," the Swedish poet exclaims: "Don't be ashamed to be a human being, be proud! / Inside you one vault after another opens endlessly. / You'll never be complete, and that's as it should be." Perhaps this is one of the great reminders that therapeutic thought has to offer us; the self is a work in progress, in the midst of perpetually transforming circumstances. Representation of the "unfinishedness" of phenomena, and also of feeling and thought, is a challenge that seems worthy for twenty-first century art. The system that pretends to be comprehensive is a dangerous thing.

The poetic use of psychology is most enriching and authentic when it is used to explore, but not resolve, the mysteries of soul and world. It takes great art to open and not to quickly confine the case of the human condition. Again, we can turn to a Tranströmer poem, "Streets of Shanghai," translated by Samuel Charters, which exhibits the benefits of the psychological legacy, but goes beyond them as well. Here are the closing images, once more focused on the pedestrian traffic on the street:

Behind each one walking here hovers a cross that wants to
    catch up to us, pass us, join us.
Something that wants to sneak up on us from behind and
    cover our eyes and whisper, "Guess who?"

We look almost happy out in the sun, while we bleed to
    death from wounds we know nothing about.

Tranströmer's poignant closing images mingle together the hard-won understandings of psychology, religion, myth, and philosophy. In doing so, the poem reveals one premise held in common by all of these systems: that we live only on the top layer of our lives. The narratives we tell ourselves, and the faces we show to the world, are not the entirety of the picture. Rather, we cohabit and collaborate with other dimensions, spiritual and psychic, which thrive behind the stage, outside the frame. Our respectful attention to those forces has the potential to enlarge and lend our lives meaning. To be unfinished, to concede that our consciousness is partial and in progress, can be construed as a cause for anxiety or as a positive excitement. It can provoke a sense of shame, or of adventure. Someplace between science and theology, perhaps through the creative activity called art, there is room for an experiment in which we are already involved: the task of fashioning what could be called a human being.

Ceremony and Discrimination

Two Muscles of Poetry

> The force that pulses
> in the boughs of trees
> and in the sap of plants
> also inhabits poems
> but it's calm there
> —Adam Zagajewski

1. The Power of Poetic Ceremony

There's an interesting moment in the middle of W. S. Merwin's poem, "The Wine," a narrative lyric which recounts the story of carrying a case of wine up a mountain trail, perhaps in preparation for a party. "With what joy I am carrying / a case of wine up a mountain," the poem begins, and a few lines later:

> it is wine that I will not drink
> I will not drink it not I
> this wine

What is going on here? The speaker has broken away from the grammatically clear narrative path and is abruptly engaged in a kind of singsong chant. And the meaning itself is nonsensical. Why would a person carry such a burden if he is not to profit in its consumption? From the forward momentum of sensible narrative, the reader has been detoured into a small sound loop, or echo chamber of song.

The poetic impact of these three lines is, for a moment, to pluck us out of time. The wending repetitive grammar works, neurologically, to transport us into an altered state of awareness. That altered state, in turn, hints suggestively at a larger context. This wine suddenly seems to be more than we had believed it to be—and the speaker, it turns out, is less central to the narrative than we had thought. Something sacred is afoot, something like a prayer. We are being initiated, in this brief passage, into a ceremonial metabolism, a kind of trance.

More and more often in recent years, I've come to notice how many poems are actually built on top of a ritual template, or partly improvised on an instinct for ceremony. That invocation of deep collective rhythms might be created in a musical way, as it is in Merwin's poem, or it might be elicited through the mysterious intellect of imagery, but, when well done, such a ceremonial element can impart to a poem unusual power and authority.

A maker may not even be conscious of this ritual dimension to her poem. Yet the slowing down and restructuring of time that occurs in ceremonies, both poetical and cultural, is something we human beings deeply crave. It isn't just truth we want from poems, nor beauty, but also this descent into a distinctly different psychic region than the one we are concerned with in daily life. The poem is our escort, or our stairway downwards into that old place. Immersed as we are in the speedy, trash-strewn torrent of contemporary life, our thirst for such formal sanctuary may be greater than ever.

Retrospectively, we can see that this thirst for the metabolism of ritual was one of the reasons why our grandparents went so bonkers for T. S. Eliot. It wasn't just the fractured existentialism of *The Waste Land* that spoke to them, it was the sonic pattern of liturgy; it was the ghost of religion still alive in Eliot's longing and nostalgia; it was the smell of recently extinguished incense.

> At the still point of the turning world. Neither flesh nor
>   fleshless;
> Neither from nor towards; at the still point, there the dance
>   is,
> But neither arrest nor movement. And do not call it fixity,
> Where past and future are gathered. Neither movement
>   from nor towards,

Neither ascent nor decline. Except for the point, the still
    point,
There would be no dance, and there is only the dance.

Eliot's passage hardly promises the reader a safe or reliable—
i.e., a divinely ordered—universe, and yet the poem conjures a
sense of orientation and location. Like much of the *Four Quartets*, from which this is drawn, this passage offers poetic instructions, which point the listener towards that still point in time; a
place that, however slippery and transient it might be, tastes of
the eternal. This slowing down and going down takes us from
the conscious realm where egotism tells us that self-gratification
is the goal—into another kind of time, which reconnects us, and
re-collects us into the shared symbolic life that is community.
Secular individualism, it turns out, has limits when it comes to
the health of the human soul, because it maroons its citizens
inside the small self, and inside a culture designed to divert and
serve that self. Jung says, "When we fell off the roof of the medieval church, we fell from the soul into the self."

Modern neurosis is the baffled side effect of being disconnected from the depths. In the twentieth century, psychotherapy was invented to address that disconnection—to do the work
of connecting the surface to the depths. But how could therapy
take the place of something like the Navajo Night Chant?

House made of dawn.
House made of evening light.
House made of the dark cloud.
House made of male rain.
House made of dark mist.
House made of female rain.
House made of pollen.
House made of grasshoppers.
Dark cloud is at the door.

The trail out of it is dark cloud.
The zigzag lightning stands high upon it.
An offering I make.
Restore my feet for me.
Restore my legs for me.

Restore my body for me.
Restore my mind for me.
Restore my voice for me.
This very day take out your spell for me.

Orientation is, in some sense, the function of every ceremony and ritual, poetry included. A poem-ritual like "The Night Chant" restores the cardinal points of earth and clarifies the place of the individual in that universe. To a postmodern person, the Navajo Night Chant may seem to be broadcasting from very far away, but the poem's situating power and poignancy is still palpable.

This ritual element is a fundamental source of poetic potency. When, as contemporary poets, we forget, and allow this primary power to fall into neglect and disuse, we forgo an important poetic resource. "The recovery of depth," says James Hollis, "will never come through an act of intellect." "It is not easy," says James Hillman, "to drop from the self into the soul." That descent is the function of communal ritual.

2. The Discriminating Intellect

Powerful as it is, ceremony is obviously not everything in poetry. If a poem had only a ritual or ceremonial dimension, it would not be a contemporary poem. It would be a prayer, or a song, whose main purpose is a kind of enchantment. A contemporary poem must do more than draw us down into the form of ritual communion, as valuable and useful as that experience may be; it must twist and sting a little. It must acknowledge modernity. It must elicit and provoke the listener's individual alertness.

A contemporary poem doesn't stop at saying, "We are in this together," but also asks, "Is there anyone awake here?" It elicits such wakefulness. This may be one difference between the genres of sacred and secular art. The former mutes individuality. The latter demands the participation and self-reliance of the reader.

Confronted with the challenge to discriminate, the reader or listener is charged to marshal together his or her own experiential knowledge, and to compare the claims of the poem against that body of experience—a feat of correlation, independent analysis, consent, or dispute.

How does this work in contemporary practice? What does a poem of such doubled intentions look like? Consider "Earth" by Katie Peterson, which joins a ritual, ceremonial element with an element of challenging discrimination:

> I didn't come here to make speeches.
> I didn't come to make trouble.
> I didn't come here to be
> somebody's mother.
> I didn't come here to make friends.
> I didn't come here to teach.
> I didn't come here to drag the space heater
> from the house in summer with an extension
> cord out to the orchard because
> the peach trees we planted
> in a climate that couldn't take them
> didn't thrive, couldn't sweeten
> their fruit in a place like this.

In the chanting declarative refrain of the first six sentences, "I didn't come here to" we can easily recognize the structure of ritual speech—not just in its formal properties, but in its content as well. Peterson's lines carry us into a rhetorical framework that possesses a mythical flavor, which exceeds the standard contemporary context of an individual speaker's unhappiness.

Rather, the poem gradually becomes identifiable as the song of a human being disentangling herself from the chains of obligation and traditional human expectation—motherhood, companionship, service, etc. It might not be too much to claim that this speaker is a kind of female Buddha-figure, chanting a song of detachment from the world. As the song goes on, it gains momentum, and we are swept up in a ceremony of divestment—a progressive self-liberation, conducted in public. We feel the heady excitement of witnessing a performance of freedom—a freedom which we could wish for ourselves: "I didn't come here to make friends. / I didn't come here to teach."

The second half of Peterson's poem enacts a different kind

of drama: when it shifts from the rhetorical to the psychological, the reader is challenged not just to respond, but to think. The development comes upon us in a grammatically stealthy manner, transforming what was a lyric refrain into a narrative about dragging a heater into an orchard:

> I didn't come here to drag the space heater
> from the house in summer with an extension
> cord out to the orchard because
> the peach trees we planted
> in a climate that couldn't take them
> didn't thrive, couldn't sweeten
> their fruit in a place like this.

In this second phase of the poem, we suddenly find ourselves not in the rhetorical realm of forceful ritual assertion, but in a narrative world of particular individual experience. We are given to infer that the speaker of the poem really did perform the act of trying to save the peach trees. The extreme extension of the sentence and its elaborate details come to signify the ambivalence and anguish of the speaker. Renunciation may still be the overt content of the exclamation, but we can discern that the effort to save the trees was a passionately sincere one on the part of our narrator. We recognize that this drama of the trees was not a negative, but an affirmative engagement with the greater world outside the self. The speaker's fierce renunciatory voice has become a psychological and attached one.

Thus, we come to recognize something new about our speaker. No longer is she a mythic feminine figure, shedding the trappings of mortal existence as she prepares to go back to the other land. Rather, she is a fallible, solitary human being who has made an emotional effort in the world, has been unsuccessful, and disappointed.

Peterson's poem looks simple on the surface, but its power comes from its two-part thrust: the compelling ritual atmosphere created by the first pattern, and the challenge of analysis, insight, and revision required by the second element, the personal narrative. The poem's "test" of the reader is that it shifts realms; it elicits a reversal of our understanding.

One might claim that the poem "Earth," in the sequential parts of its consciousness, embodies the psychological narrative that is called the hero's journey, or sometimes called the journey of individuation. It enacts the journey away from home, then the return.

Another poem which combines elements of ceremony and challenge is "The Work" by Allen Grossman. Grossman is one of the great vatic American poets of the mid-twentieth century. Aesthetically, he is a child of Wallace Stevens, and a cousin to Allen Ginsberg. His oracular sensibility probably cost him inclusion in the contemporary canon, but Grossman is a poet who never considers writing about less than the most serious human matters:

A great light is the man who knows the woman he loves

A great light is the woman who knows the man she loves

And carries the light into room after room arousing
The sleepers and looking hard into the face of each
And then sends them asleep again with a kiss
Or a whole night of love

                        and goes on and on until
The man and woman who carry the great lights of the
Knowledge of the one lover enter the room

                            toward which
Their light is sent and fit the one and the other torch
In a high candelabrum and there is such light
That children leap up

                      unless the sea swallow them
In the crossing or hatred or war against which do not
Pray only but be vigilant and set your hand to the work.

Here again we can feel the poetic strength of ceremonial invocation—Grossman's speech is ritual and biblical in cadence. "The Work" employs the voice, imagery, rhetoric, and syntax of the psalmist. The rhythm of the poem is one part of its tidal persuasion. In it, we hear not the voice of Allen Grossman, but the prophetic authority of Yahweh, sanctifying and unfolding the mystery of earthly life, and the mission of man and woman together in the world. We are anointed by and wrapped in its authority.

Its grammatically additive syntax—and, and, and—and the hyperbolic-extension of the poem's second sentence also persuade us that this is a passionate and powerful speaker, reciting the allegory of the original mother and father, and that all shall be well.

Something unexpected happens in the last three lines of Grossman's poem, however, which wakes us from our trustful trance. This last development of the poem, initiated by the word "unless," thrusts responsibility like a torch back into the hands of the auditor. It is not a reassurance, but a warning and command: "be vigilant and set your hand to the work." The parental and heroic figures of the poem are powerful in their sponsorship, yet their authority can go just so far. Conditions in the world are unpredictable—seas swallow children, hatred exists, in a world of profane dangers you must guard yourselves and your loved ones.

If the fierce, defiant opening of Peterson's poem is transformed into a vulnerable account of personal dismay, similarly, Grossman's poem changes from a benediction into a cautionary political admonition. But both poems surprise us with how they turn and call us back into a condition of alertness—which seems a requirement for a contemporary poem.

When a poem possesses ritual intelligence, its resonance extends beyond the framework of the personal anecdote. It catches our interest as readers because, consciously or unconsciously, we recognize that the gesture of the poem is, in part, a cultural dispensation. Apology, farewell, accusation, defense, commemoration of a birth or a death, pledge of loyalty, prayer for protection, declaration of family values—these occasions are compass points of human existence. In every culture and time, they are the seeds at the center of songs and stories. Such occasions have an innate strength as the material of poetry.

The contemporary poet who wishes to harness that power will start to see that occasions for poetry surround us. When I turn my key in the lock of my apartment, I am performing a symbolic act as well as a practical one. When my sister feeds her cat, or takes it to be euthanized at the vet's, a very old contract is being enacted. When one undresses for the first time for a lover, that is a ceremony. When the parent walks through the house late at night, turning off lights and checking locks, it is an act as ceremonial as a genuflection. It is all a kind of taking of communion. The poet who possesses the instinct to detect such sacraments can find a poem almost anywhere.

Here's one more example of the ceremonial instinct in a contemporary poem by Patrick Donnelly. The occasion of the poem? The speaker is turning over his house to new buyers. It is a moment of sharpened awareness and lyric potential. Will he issue a benediction, or a curse? Is he grief-stricken or liberated by this cutting loose from home? The moment is at once a station of the cross, a passing, and a going forth. The poem is called "Note to the New Owner":

Because you toured the house with the termite inspector,
baby in your arms, your mother in tow, then out the door
without speaking to me—to me! who had watched my face
age twelve years in these mirrors—I determined

to root every living thing out of the garden—*my* garden,
that I created *ex nihilo*, that I nursed in sour shade
between shards of broken grass, that I made and now revoke,
breaking every bleeding heart and fiddleneck.

Your mother gasped with delight at forced branches
flowering in a glass bowl in the kitchen. She, at least, is a
person.
For her sake I leave the forsythia to explode each spring.

As it turns out, "Note" is more a malediction than a blessing: a judgment is issued and a punishment is promised. Feeling slighted, ignored, already erased, the speaker swears to destroy the garden he has loved. In effect, he casts a blight on the life of his successor.

Donnelly is a highly conscious craftsperson, and the ceremonial nature of the account is signified by strong cadence throughout the poem: You can feel the strong iambic pulse—

"that I made and now revoke"—and in that authoritative pulse, we feel the public certainty of a decided mind. As witnesses and listeners, we are subordinated to and entranced by the trial and execution of the sentence.

Not until line nine do we find a divergence in the poem's ceremonial agenda, an opening of heart, when, at the last minute, the speaker decides to leave the forsythia for the mother of his adversary—an act of discrimination and mercy on his part ("she, at least, is a person"). As God allows Lot to leave Gomorrah, and permits Noah to survive the devastating deluge, mercy is granted. Yet even this concession is couched in ambivalent and paradoxical terms; in springtime, we are told, the forsythia will "explode."

If it seems far-fetched to propose that ancient cultural stories—those of Noah, or Lot—inform and empower Donnelly's domestic narrative, remember that this is how myth works. In the deep reservoir of psychic shapes, the archetypal narratives brood and circulate, enriching and charging the particular plot with significance and depth. The mother gasps, and spring springs. Neurologically, the old waters turn and surge inside these contemporary plots and contexts. If the poem has been skillfully made, and engaged the deep structures of human culture, art is electrified by myth and consciousness. Then it becomes art capable of changing our vision, our behavior, maybe our lives.

What These Ithakas Mean

Some Thoughts about Metaphor and Questing

> Keep Ithaka always in your mind.
> Arriving there is what you're destined for.
> But don't hurry the journey at all.
> Better if it lasts for years.
>   —C. P. Cavafy

1. Homer's Metaphors

Blind Homer, famous for his two great narrative poems, is also famous for his metaphors. In fact, the metaphors that populate the *Iliad* and *Odyssey* are so stylistically distinct that they are *called* Homeric metaphors. They have the special status of being their own genre.

Homer's metaphors are impressive for many reasons: for their cinematic vividness, their sweep and lucidity, their seemingly effortless elaborations. For the way that they fabricate whole alternative narrative scenes inside the larger poem without interrupting and derailing the forward momentum of the main narrative.

But the quality of Homer's metaphors is especially visible in the way that they establish multiple points of correspondence between the A term and the elongated or amplified B term. In a Homeric metaphor, the correspondences between referent and image are complexly, brilliantly *thorough*.

For example, here is how Homer, in the *Odyssey* (translated by Robert Fagles), represents Penelope's relation to the suitors who surround her:

Her mind in torment, wheeling
like some lion at bay, dreading gangs of hunters
closing their cunning ring around him for the finish.

Every metaphor presents an equation between an A term and a B term. In this case, A = Penelope's mind; B = a trapped lion cornered and surrounded by avaricious hunters. Here, Penelope's internal state is made concrete, particular, and poignant by an elaborate image.

The comparison may seem simple enough at first, but what makes the metaphor masterful is the number and complexity of the correspondences between actuality and image, and the many distinct *emphases* built into the comparison.

Penelope's helplessness and dread are two of the qualities emphasized in contrast to the predatorial—in fact, murderous—intentions of the suitors. But Penelope is not *merely* helpless—she's not being compared to a helpless little rabbit, but to a *lion*. Thus her power and nobility are also suggested by the image, and even her potential to do damage. We understand that the would-be hunters may well find themselves in danger when they mess with Penelope.

Later in the *Odyssey*, in Book 22 (translation by Robert Fitzgerald), a similarly elaborate image—of those same suitors after they have been slaughtered by Odysseus—occurs in the banquet hall. Again, we can admire the meticulous patience embodied in the writing, the pace and particularity of detail Homer expends on his metaphor:

Think of a catch that fishermen haul in to a halfmoon bay
in a fine-meshed net from the white-caps of the sea:
how all are poured out on the sand, in throes for the salt sea,
twitching their cold lives away in Helios' fiery air:
so lay the suitors heaped on one another.

Now who is helpless, pathetic, dying, anonymous, and confused? The suitors, their lives spilled out on the floor, are in "throes," convulsing in the "fiery air" and they are no longer distinguished by individual names, but lie in a wordless heap. It is almost as if the latter metaphor exacts revenge upon the culprits featured in the earlier metaphor. The suitors have been transformed from eager, merciless hunters into cold, dead fish.

2. Culture Building

In metaphors like the above, Homer's exquisite discipline is evident in his ability to handle such rich pictorial asides without losing the forward momentum of his central narrative. Another less obvious dimension of such Homeric metaphors is their relation not just to the text in which they are embedded, but to the culture at large that once surrounded them.

Homer's metaphors are unobtrusive acts of what could be called *culture binding*. Even when describing scenes of violence, destruction, war, or great storms, Homer's metaphors assert the ultimate unity of Greek culture, its unfragmented wholeness. Even though his stories may depict moments of extreme uncertainty and apparent chaos, they nonetheless also insinuate the coherence and deep stability of the society they are describing.

How so? Homeric metaphors do the work of culture-binding by invoking, in their description, images of more "normal" activities than war or adventure.

When, for example, the suitors are compared to a haul of caught fish, or when Penelope's dilemma is compared to a hunting expedition, Homer is, in a way, reassuring the audience that the other dimensions of common human life continue to exist. Even in tumultuous times, the poet is asserting that fishing and hunting, as much as war, are perpetual institutions of their own and, collectively, they knit the world together.

Thus Homer's extended metaphors, for all their far-flung imagination, nonetheless keep their world organized. Homer is, after all, a *classical* writer, and in classical writing, both the human mind and the universe are represented as an ordered place. In fact, the logic and clarity of the speaker's speech itself is a reflection of the great, well-ordered civilization that it belongs to. Homer's sentences, his story, his faith in social codes and ethics are all under his control. They may be embellished by wild, muscular, lusciously detailed metaphors, but those metaphors themselves are not *unruly*—they are biddable. In the overall narrative of the *Odyssey*, the hero is headed towards home, a reunion and a marriage; towards love, healthy cattle, good sex, a full belly, and closure. And, even in its individual metaphors, by this kind of knitting or binding, the writer's assertion of faith in culture is embodied.

For its original listeners and for readers since, the poem's underlying, palpable confidence in the unshakable stability of the human realm must have served as a kind of verification. Listening to these narratives chanted in a hall flickering with torch light, the Homeric audience must have felt that their world was complete and whole, inclusive of pleasure and peace as well as war. The universe in which they lived had rules and hierarchies—it had, you could say, enduring meaning.

In Book 9 (translation by Robert Fagles), when Odysseus and his men decide to put out the eye of the Cyclops, we encounter another Homeric metaphor which performs this act of cultural reassurance, even in its depiction of horrific violence. We are told how, after the giant has fallen asleep, the Greek warriors sharpen a length of olive wood into a point and harden it in the fire; then, when the Cyclops is asleep, they drive it into his one large eye and turn it in the crater of that eye socket, to blind him. It is a marvelously ruthless act, and the poet allows it a fulsome, graphic unfurling:

> as a shipwright bores his beam with a shipwright's drill
> that men below, whipping the strap back and forth, whirl
> and the drill keeps twisting faster, never stopping—
> So we seized our stake with its fiery tip
> and bored it round and round in the giant's eye

A horrific act indeed, yet the comparison Homer employs for the brutal blinding is drawn from a peaceable trade, that of the shipwright, a boat builder, and the analogy expresses a detailed knowledge of how such a craftsman uses his awl to make a hole into which a peg shall be inserted to bind the planks of the ship together. On some subliminal level, the suggestion exists that even this violent act is normal, that such acts are necessary to hold the fabric of culture itself together.

Just a few lines later, that message is reiterated by reference to another homely trade. The sharpened wooden stake sizzles and hisses in the eye-socket of the Cyclops, Homer says, like a piece of hot metal being cooled in water at a blacksmith's shop:

> as a blacksmith plunges a glowing ax or adze
> in an ice-cold bath and the metal screeches steam
> and its temper hardens . . .
> so the eye of the Cyclops sizzled round that stake!

Such comparisons are not just spectacularly graphic; in their circuitous way they also assert the continuity and coherence of the domestic world ongoing around the *Odyssey*'s glamorous adventures. They imply that shipwrights and blacksmiths are engaged in their proper livelihoods, the activities that make peacetime a smooth-running sort of business, where people know their jobs and do them skillfully. Homer implies that, just over the hill from the battle, someone is gathering warm eggs from beneath hens, and making sail cloth, and catching fish, or herding goats. Life is still intact.

Homer's poem can thus be viewed not just as a great yarn, but as a system of scaffolding intended to retain and uphold images of order and civilization. On one level at least, Homer's great metaphors are made to keep everything bound together; to show the intricate hierarchical cohesiveness of the world.

3. Jumping Out of the Boat

Let it be said, however, that an entirely different school of metaphor exists. In contrast to Homer's elaborate, classically-orchestrated metaphors, sometimes metaphor is *not* used primarily to illuminate a preceding object or abstraction. Sometimes poetic metaphors or images are so strange or sensational, so wild and distracting and *unruly* that they displace and overpower their point of departure, their referent, the A term. When that happens, a metaphor may *break* narrative or discourse. Such metaphorical procedures don't bind culture rationally together, but unbind and disrupt it.

This is the kind of metaphor or image that Robert Bly

called the *leaping image,* an image that is not dedicated to the preservation of culture but, in a way, to the breaking open of rationality;the exposure and expressiveness of the raw inner life.

Here's an example from an early poem by Bly, when he was under the influence of the leaping, image-centered poetry of Spanish surrealism:

Our spirit is inside the baseball rising into the light.

So the crippled ships go out into the deep,
sexual orchids fly out to meet the rain,
   the singer sings from deep in his chest, . . .
the eyes of the nation go blind.

The building across the street suddenly explodes,
wild horses run through the long hair on the ground floor.
Cripple Creek's survivors peer out from an upper-story
   window, blood pours from their ears,
the Sioux dead sleep all night in the rain troughs on the
   Treasury Building.
                   "Condition of the Working Classes: 1970"

This vision—in its performance, if not its content—is far from the Homeric one; it is anarchic, passionate, furious, and sequenced like a series of firecrackers; it scrambles resemblance and narrative together. Next to it, Homeric metaphors look very precisely controlled and careful, very *civilized* as they are.

In his essays, Bly often compares poetic imagery to a creature or beast, an organic entity with a will of its own, and a kind of healthy unpredictability. Leaping poetry values irrationality over rationality, and disproportion rather than proportion. The theoretical orientation here—the relationship of the artist to the imagination—could be said to be mainly Jungian; not *mastering,* but receptive and expressive. Leaping poetry is not interested in culture binding or flawless control of its materials, but in the eruptions of the unconscious into language and consciousness—a kind of wakeful dreaming.

Let me offer another example of the unruly extended metaphor, from a contemporary Algerian-Arab poet named Venus Khoury-Gata, translated by Marilyn Hacker:

Once upon a time she had a book
with lines which ran from east to west like Siberian trains
Black smoke escaped from the pages when the phrases
    pulled out of the station
some of them shoved each other
others let themselves be stepped over by the ones who'd
    decided
to reach the words The End before nightfall

It was an indoor book
which never went out for fear that malicious winds would fill
    it with sadness
It recognized the woman by her scent of ink and cumin

She laughed with it
slept with it
her finger groping in the dark of the alphabet . . .

You *might* say that this is ever so slightly like a Homeric metaphor, in that it has an A and a B term. Khoury-Gata's poem, it
could be said, compares the experience of reading a book to a
train ride. However, at the end of the poem, do we understand
the act of reading any better, or "see" a book better for the comparison? No, not really, and that's not the point.

Rather we are simply delighted by the poet's adventurous de-
familiarization, the oddity and the ingenuity of Khoury-Gata's
comparisons. In fact, we are in some sense delighted by the *inac-
curacies* or *misalignments* of the comparison, the ways in which a
book is preposterously *unlike* a train ride. Such a metaphorical
style does not illuminate the world of actuality, but invents and
wanders in an alternative world.

The metaphor here commissions the reader with quite a different cognitive task from the one Homer asks of us. Khoury-Gata's
aesthetic is like taking a puff of medical marijuana to loosen the
brain. Such imaginative play stretches and relaxes the mind from
the constraints of its rational bindings, its pragmatisms, its obliga-
tions to the real. We go along with such metaphors for a different
reason than the reason we read along with Homer. Khoury-Gata's
poem pursues a wholly different cognitive agenda, a different species and metaphysic of metaphor making.

This loosening and disorientation is one reason why we value the associative imagination—and it is why we need and reward its practitioners with our affectionate attention—for their looseness, for their freedom of disorientation. Not everything, such poetics assert, has to be "good" for something!

4. Disorientation as an End in Itself

In this way, you can see, some metaphors, and some metaphor-making sensibilities, are interested in using the device of the metaphor, not as a form of *illustration*—employed to illuminate or to exemplify—but to *disorient*, to feed strange sugar to the mind. Disorientation as an end in itself can certainly be an entertaining activity but, in mysterious ways, it may also be a psychically valuable activity.

Such metaphors, it must be said, may have a built-in limitation when it comes to sustained thinking. Their sensationalism often has a disruptive effect. You could say that they are "insubordinate," like a hyperactive child who upsets the entire classroom. They may be highly entertaining, but they are also unbalancing, making it difficult for the poem to complete a thought. When such exotic comparisons appear, they may steal all the reader's attention away from the referent, the A term. When Richard Brautigan, for instance, says that "She was as crazy as a rubber duck in a tornado," we may simply forget what we were talking about, stopped in our tracks by that strange image.

Likewise, when Denis Johnson says, in one of his poems, "and then I see it rising, on the horizon, that gigantic yellow warrant / for my arrest, one sixth the size of the earth—I'm talking of course about the moon," we might find ourselves no longer really thinking about the moon. Or when the poet Jeff McDaniels says that "The crack smoke entered my brain / like Stalin pushing out from between his mother's legs," we may find our attention has wandered elsewhere, temporarily demented.

When imagination operates in this disruptive mode, drunken and whirling, it is commonly referred to as the Dionysian temperament at work. Ask, if you like, "Well, what is the *purpose* of such metaphors? What is the *usefulness* of metaphors that don't clarify the world? That don't really contribute to either story or meaning-making?"

Yet Dionysius has his ancient place in culture too. His is the figure that rides into the city on a donkey, and intoxicates it, and reminds it how to dance once more. Is it possible to claim that such art, in a highly pragmatic society, may act as a cultural corrective, pushing back against the pressure to only create objects that are *useful*, or economically "valued?" In that way, metaphor-practitioners like Khoury-Gata or Brautigan can be seen as both anti-capitalistic and anti-Puritanical.

In other words, the spontaneous wildness of some images and metaphors in a poem is a method of yielding control to the imagination. That is the constitutional difference between a writer whose aim is overseeing and orchestrating the comprehensive work of art and another kind of writer who is interested in adventure and disruption.

Decide which style of imagination you prefer and you might just learn something about yourself. Or maybe you are a person who likes both styles, both sushi and French fries, but not at the same time.

5. The Disorientation Device of the Ghazal

Many Middle-Eastern poems, especially those belonging to the Persian-Sufi tradition, practice a disorientation aesthetic which is on the one hand wild and anarchic, but paradoxically also very purposeful.

Through the power of image, speed, paradox, and leaping, the ghazal form aims not to organize, but to overwhelm the mind; to loosen the fist of rationality and make the mind unclench, shed its agenda of sensemaking, and look into a bigger kind of mystery behind or hidden among the assertions of the couplets. Ghazals are a poetic mode dedicated to *unbinding*; the freedom they can elicit is often equated with ecstasy, like that of a bird getting out of its cage.

One aspect of the ghazal technique is the way it bombards the listener with a profusion of image and paradox. Here are some couplets from a poem of Hafez "The Guesthouse with Two Doors," translated by Robert Bly and Leonard Lewisohn:

The red rose has broken open, and the nightingale
Is drunk. You Sufis who love each moment
Freed from time, this amounts to a call to joy.

The bedrock of our famous repentance seemed
To be tough as granite. Look, the delicate
Glass cup has split the repentance at the first blow.

Offer us wine, because in the court of God's
Magnificence, what difference is there between the Prince
And a cop, between the sober man and the drunk?

We travelers live in the guesthouse with two doors,
And we must leave. Who cares if your life goes on
Underneath a big dome or a small one?

The waiting station of pleasure and delight
Always includes suffering. In Pre-Eternity
Our souls all bound themselves to that tragedy.

The images and figurative speech of a ghazal arrive so swiftly, so declaratively, and in such profusion, that the mind, try as it might, cannot collate, analyze and integrate them into the form of a unitary argument. A ghazal like this is so rich in images and metaphors that it won't hold still long enough to make sense of.

To go back to our original description of what a metaphor is—an A term equated with a B term—here the A term is never explicitly identified. We wander through a vocabulary so loose in its symbolic contents that we seem to have left the shore of sensemaking behind. Overwhelmed, but entertained, the rational mind is pushed into a state of paralysis, and the surprising result is that intelligence is freed from itself.

The red rose has broken open, and the nightingale
Is drunk. . . .

Offer us wine because in the court of God's
Magnificence, what difference is there between the Prince
And a cop, between the sober man and the drunk?

Think back to the Homeric metaphors with which this essay began, and consider how coherently organized they are, how orderly and paced, such that the reader or listener does not forget the actual event with which the image is placed in parallel. The pleasure of the Homeric metaphor is to collate the referent with the imagistic comparison and to relish the precision of the many correspondences.

But in a ghazal, you get an A term, then an E term, a D term, and a Z term; a sequence so scrambled and fast-paced, it is impossible to collate and organize. The ghazal breaks down the hierarchy of orderly presentation, and the result is a kind of ecstatic delirium of intuition.

Such poetics stimulate levels of intuition in us that the rest of the human world undervalues. Behind the analytical brain there is a "feeling-mind" that has an anatomy of meanings and a hunger of its own. Instead of defending institutions, and the glories of the civilized world, such poetry defends intuitions and celebrates the wild potential of the undomesticated individual mind.

Is a ghazal "culture-binding"? No—in fact, if the essence of culture is organization, a good ghazal is culture-demolishing. If the ghazal is meant to be liberating, it is concerned not with maintaining social order, but with liberating only one individual mind at a time from, some would say, the straightjacket of cultural paradigms. Cognitively, the ghazals of Ghalib or Hafez are engaged in a very different business than the Homeric methods of metaphor.

6. The Heart of the Discussion

When we distinguish between these two modes of metaphor-making, we arrive at an old and essential difference of opinion about the purpose of art. Perhaps it is a difference in individual temperament, about what poetic language is supposed to *do*. Perhaps it is an argument about whether the imagination itself should be orienting or disorienting—culture-binding or mind-unravelling? Should metaphor place things into proportion and ground us, and assert the relatedness of all things? Or should it entertain and dishevel us?

William Butler Yeats's poem "The Second Coming" offers one of the most memorable and frequently-cited images of the twentieth century: "Turning and turning in the widening gyre / The falcon cannot hear the falconer; / Things fall apart; the centre cannot hold . . ."

Yeats's allegorical image has been presented thousands of times as an ominous metaphorical prediction of the end-of-civilization, the impending consequences of modernity. Unity and coherence have been stretched and finally broken; we are now all fragments flying outwards away from each other. Our human mastery of the world, which here might be signified by the relationship between the hunter and his falcon, has fallen apart. Our tools no longer work, and the bird cannot hear us, nor can we hear the bird. We have broken with nature and with order.

Yeats's image also provides a trope for the two types of metaphorical style—what might be called the *centripetal* and the *centrifugal* style. One kind of poetic instinct, the centripetal, is committed to holding things in their orbit around a central core. Another poetic mode, the centrifugal, embodies the energy that flies outward, straining to break away from the center and to escape its orbit, to go seeking new information in the realms of the unknown.

Metaphor is the powerful instrument used by both enterprises, a device that can be adapted to reflect the nature of those different agendas. One kind of poet uses metaphor to bind, order, and reconnect the parts of culture; another allows the parts to fly apart in different directions at great velocity, with a kind of randomness; to be deranged.

Another way to generally characterize the difference between these two styles of poetic imagination is to say that one school uses images as a *tool*, and that the other uses imagery as a device for *divination*, as a kind of *oracle* or crystal ball; or a well, into which you lower your bucket, intent on allowing this deep aquifer of image and primal intelligence to communicate.

One style of metaphor assumes a stance of purposeful mastery on the part of the maker; the other assumes a position of supplication, receptiveness, and humility—even perhaps a desire to be overmastered.

We know that the professions of dream analysis and of Jungian psychology tend to see images as a means to divine the unknown depths of the psyche. For the members of this tribe, whatever rises out of the depths of the unconscious comes from an intelligent source that is beyond the horizon of the conscious egoistic mind. These images and figures and stories provide us with information that we could not reach through rational and analytical avenues. This is what Freud called the "royal road to the unconscious," a path open to those willing enough to step forward into conversation with their own ignorance.

Which is the more vital function for art to play?
To bring us to our senses or to take us out of them?

One question for us postmoderns is to ask whether we live in a culture that is so pulled apart psychologically, economically, racially, and technologically that we can no longer sustain our belief in Homeric-style metaphors, or trust stories which will speak to all of us and, in a sense, bind us together.

If that were true, we might advance to the next question and ask, "Where are the images that perfectly depict the contemporary state of the soul? What is the image that will show us to ourselves, or the image that will offer us the solace of seeing our plight clearly?"

As a believer in language and in the mysterious intelligence of the unconscious, I wonder if we can make a request of the realm of the metaphor: can we ask it to give us a figure for our plight, our human condition, our postmodern dis-ease?

7. Exhaustion: But What Is the Metaphor for Postmodernity? For the Feeling of the Self in Our Time? For America?

All this talk talk talk talk talk.

Sometimes it seems there is an agony behind all this eloquence, all this articulate, analytical intellect. Sometimes, doesn't it seem that the more we talk, the further away from truth we get?

And, after all, isn't there is a proper time to shut up?
A time when creativity is fallow and flat and useless, or
  worse?
A point in life when you come to the end of your exhausted
  understanding?

When you are young, such cul-de-sacs tend to be, and seem, personal: You have begun to suspect that the story you memorized as a child, or the one you have been telling to yourself for years, is not working. It is untrue, or misguided, or self-serving and, using it as your compass, you have nowhere further to go.

When we are older, perhaps, we may similarly feel that the story of our culture doesn't work; that Western history, and Western values, and human nature somehow have not been properly configured, they are malformed. You feel that, not only is the story not working, but even the language of your *diagnosis* for the problem feels stale and tired. You stand at the end of the road and see no way forward. To continue talking seems itself nothing more than a vain distraction, a false pretense.

This is the moment in life's pilgrimage of which Eliot says in "The Four Quartets,"

I said to my soul, be still, and wait without hope
For hope would be hope for the wrong thing; wait without
  love
For love would be love of the wrong thing; there is yet faith
But the faith and the love and the hope are all in the
  waiting.
Wait without thought, for you are not ready for thought:
So the darkness shall be the light, and the stillness the
  dancing.

Eliot is, paradoxically, talking about the importance of *not* trying to make a story; the necessity of letting go of the story you have been attached to and keep attempting to resurrect; about standing still and looking for signs rather than manufacturing them out of exhausted material; not grasping, spastically, for a way forward. It is a sense of knowing when you need help from a source outside your typical means.

The idea has often been offered as a kind of comfort, that history repeats itself; that what is happening now has happened many times before; that there is nothing new under the sun; that we should therefore be patient and keep faith. Ice Ages and Dark Ages of many kinds have visited us before. This is not the first time in human history when people's minds have been disconnected from their bodies, or when we have been unable to know what we are feeling. It has all happened before.

But maybe that wisdom is untrue. Maybe this moment, this contemporary condition of which we are the fingertip, this precise flavor of disassociation *is* unique; maybe it has never existed before.

At this point, you think, the right metaphor might help us out. But where will it come from, and what is it? The right image could show us our way through, could provide a figure for our postmodern distress. If we cannot figure it, image it, or metaphor it, we have no power to move. If we don't have a solution, then at least a good *diagnosis*—like the image of that falcon turning in the gyre—would be a comfort around which we could gather.

Or maybe it is appropriate that we should acknowledge our poverty of image, of idea, of knowing. At certain way stations we have nothing in our imaginations, nothing clever enough or sufficiently wise. At such moments, inaction is appropriate; and so we wait and listen with humility and openness. For a modern human being, anxious and habituated to the notion of conquering our problems, what could be harder than not-knowing? Yet it may not be mastery, or ingenuity, or even metaphor that will preserve us. It may be that only listening, extended and authentic listening, will replenish our imaginations.

Cast Swine Before Pearls

Comedy, Shamanic Rage, and Poetry

When I was a young reader of poems and a consumer of giant helpings of rock and roll, I dreamed of a poem that could manifest the cleansing, eardrum-breaking fury of a rock song: *Gimme Shelter*, by the Stones; or Hendrix's dignified defiance in *All Along the Watchtower*, which turns irony into howl; or The Who's *Won't Get Fooled Again*. In those days, certainly, I thought that any poet might die happy if he or she wrote just one poem as good as a Van Morrison song, like *Listen to the Lion*.

The problem seemed to be one of *volume*; how can a poem, which relies so much on nuance and ambiguity, on insight and inflection, play really *loud*? How can it express rage that is not thuddingly numb-skulled without the thunderous support of a drum kit and a Fender bass?

Right around that time I might have encountered Kenneth Rexroth's poem, "Thou Shalt Not Kill," his elegy for Dylan Thomas, a truly furious poem that builds and builds and crescendos. Here is an excerpt from the final section:

> He is dead.
> The bird of Rhiannon.
> He is dead.
> In the winter of the heart.
> He is Dead.
> In the canyons of death,
> They found him dumb at last,
> In the blizzard of lies.
> He never spoke again.
> He died.

He is dead.
In their antiseptic hands,
He is dead.
The little spellbinder of Cader Idris.
He is dead.
The sparrow of Cardiff.
He is dead.
The canary of Swansea.
Who killed him?
Who killed the bright-headed bird?
You did, you son of a bitch.
You drowned him in your cocktail brain.
He fell down and died in your synthetic heart.
You killed him,
Oppenheimer the Million-Killer,
You killed him,
Einstein the Gray Eminence.
You killed him,
Havanahavana, with your Nobel Prize.
You killed him, General,
Through the proper channels. . . .
There is a smell of blood
In the smell of the turf smoke.
They have struck him down,
The son of David ap Gwilym.
They have murdered him,
The Baby of Taliessin.
There he lies dead,
By the Iceberg of the United Nations.
There he lies sandbagged,
At the foot of the Statue of Liberty.
The Gulf Stream smells of blood
As it breaks on the sand of Iona
And the blue rocks of Canarvon.
And all the birds of the deep sea rise up
Over the luxury liners and scream,
"You killed him! You killed him.
In your God damned Brooks Brothers suit,
You son of a bitch."

Rexroth's jeremiad, with its tight litany form and rich welter of imagery, diction, and idiom, harnesses its occasion to indict and accuse the whole twentieth century of the death of Dylan Thomas. Disproportionate? Yes, but why not? Among other things, poetry is an act of intelligent projection. "Thou Shalt Not Kill" reportedly took Rexroth twenty minutes to read in performance, and one can imagine the escalating drama towards crescendo. Reportedly it was read in 1950 with the young Allen Ginsberg seated in the audience, not long before he wrote *Howl.* How could it not have influenced him?

What humanizes the speaker's rage, what keeps the poem a poem, is the grief which colors it—we understand that the speaker's immoderation and anger come from deep personal injury. We recognize that the rage comes out of an experience of empathy, and that forcefield between love and denunciation moves us as much as Lear's rage on the mountainside. It amounts to the difference between poetic terrorism and poetic tragedy.

Yet, as truly marvelous as Rexroth's poem is, there's a simplistic quality to it that might bother us over repeated readings—its conspicuous self-righteousness foreshortens its insightfulness. The man in the Brooks Brothers suit is a wonderful figure to end on, but the disproportionate fury being unleashed upon him also makes the poem's ending slightly absurd, as well as glorious. Our poet *knows* that some poor accountant in a Madison Avenue office is not responsible for the death of the Welsh poet, but that accountant stands in for all of us, even while providing us with a target for our sweet acetylene.

In poetry right now, rage isn't always fashionably cool. The pendulum has swung a long way from oratorical Beat sincerity. In the current climate, irony and conceptual whimsy, various styles of verbal wit, and forty-four flavors of self-consciousness prevail. In many ways ours is a sophisticate era. Sincerity is required to costume itself now. In a climate of detachment and intellect, anger often seems simple-minded, self-righteous, unexamined, Cro-Magnon even. In an era when we presume—for good reasons, admittedly—our individual *powerlessness*, to get angry seems almost beside the point. Who, after all, would the rage be directed at? Because, in various ways, we recognize our own participation in the systems that enclose us; we are largely tame.

Yet anger can be powerfully functional in poetry, not just because it is an inescapable element of human nature, but because it connects us—like depression and ecstasy—with deep well-springs of instinct and intelligence. Often, anger makes poets funny. When Rexroth says, "You drowned him in your cocktail brain!" we see comedy irrepressibly sneaking in the side door of rage. And perhaps we see the act of the imagination overcoming even the speaker's pessimism.

What rage and humor have in common: they both overcome pessimism; they expel it, cast it out. When combined, they add something to each other as well. If comedy provides detachment and perceptiveness, rage provides the forcefulness of a worthy occasion, saving comedy from mere wit.

Here is the opening of another poem of rage and humor, by the contemporary Israeli poet Aharon Shabtai, translated by Peter Cole; it is as classical and vulgar as the social satires of Juvenal:

To My Friend

Apuleius, in the *Golden Ass*, writes of times like these:
A man with the head of a pig becomes king;
people mutter gibberish and turn into wolves.
Beautiful women fornicate with apes.
Rabbis shoot pistols, affix mezuzahs to a whorehouse.
Crowds drink down a rat's jokes, the hyena's howl.
New breasts are bought on the open market, one's buttocks
     are lifted.
The rich man farts and the nation stirs with excitement.
On the street, people wave flags made of money.
A journalist's tongue sticks out of his ass, and suddenly he's
     become a thinker.

Once again, imagery carries the burden of discourse: "the rich man farts and the nation stirs with excitement" is one of my favorite lines. Why? For its contempt, its ire, and its accuracy. Satire takes its edge from precision, its precise encapsulation of human nature and social manners. In the skillful comic we recognize a valuable detachment and clear-headedness. The other quality which humor lends poetry is range of motion, the flexibility of psychic freedom shown by the speaker, the variety of perspective that can be fetched and collated; unexpectedness. Shabtai gets points for both imagistic virtuosity and perceptiveness.

Among American poets, many deserve great credit for their combinations of fury and funny. Philip Levine, Galway Kinnell, Sylvia Plath, Muriel Rukeyser, Diane Wakowski, Robert Bly, Eleanor Lerman, John Berryman, Gerald Stern, Edward Field, Thomas Sayers Ellis, Denise Duhamel—all of them are capable of being angry and imaginative at the same time.

Whitman is usually too generous for misanthropy, but in section 32 of *Song of Myself,* he lets loose an uncharacteristic sarcasm, a grimace:

> I think I could turn and live with animals, they are so placid
> and self contained.
> I stand and look at them long and long.
>
> They do not sweat and whine about their condition,
> They do not lie awake in the dark and weep for their sins,
> They do not make me sick discussing their duty to God,
> Not one is dissatisfied . . . with the mania of owning
> things . . .

"They do not make me sick discussing their duty to God!" One senses the reams of experience compressed into that line, which fuses humor, despair, and contempt. Why is it funny? It's accurate! Whitman may be mean here, but his accuracy thrills us.

Into this discussion one might bring the most recent avatar of this mode: Frederick Seidel. Seidel is one of the bastards of American poetry; a rich nasty-boy poet, a sort of prankster pariah, sometimes censured for reckless endangerment of good taste; a surrealist font of unapologetic opinion. If there were an Olympic event for Extreme Poetry, Seidel might be the American entrant.

With his hostility and imperiousness, his poetic strategy of shock and awe, Seidel was post-9/11 before 9/11. Perhaps as a consequence, his work is mostly not featured in the big anthologies of the canonically viable—not the *Norton,* or the Poulin's *Contemporary American Poetry,* nor the *Postmodern American Poetry*

Anthology. Seidel, born in 1937, is a "senior poet" now in his mid-seventies, and his eight or nine books represent a major career, culminating in the publication of the trilogy, *The Cosmos.* Since then, several more new books have burst forth. Seidel is like what doctors call an "orphan disease": no research money has been raised to find a cure. But there are some valuable poetic lessons to be learned from his work.

Seidel knows, as few do, about that interface between bad taste and revelation, about the potential for poetic force inherent in the socially unacceptable. Reading certain of his poems, one feels a ripple of excitement like a breeze: shock, and at the same time, the impulse to laugh out loud. Take the beginning of "To Die For":

> The ants on the kitchen counter stampede toward ecstasy.
> The finger chases them down while the herd runs this way
>   and that way.
> They are alive while they are alive in their little way.
> They burst through their little ant outfits, which tear apart
>   rather easily.

The anthropomorphic insinuations are one thing: what makes it Seidelian is the gleeful aggressiveness of the description, coupled with the deliberately unpleasant diffidence of "their little way" and "rather easily". But if any decorum remained, in the next lines the poet performs his trademark step-too-far, in rhyme:

> The little black specks were shipped to Brazil in ships.
> The Portuguese whipped the little back specks to bits.
> The sugar plantations on the horrible tropical coast where
>   the soil was rich
> Were a most productive ant Auschwitz.

Then Seidel *continues* to complicate, prosecute, and contaminate the connotative underplot:

> The sugar bowl on the counter is a D-cup, containing one
>   large white breast.
> The breast in the bowl is covered by excited specks

That are so beyond, and running around, they are wrecks.
They just like things that are sweet. That's what they like to
  eat.

The day outside is blue and good.
God is in the neighborhood.
The nearby ocean puts liquid lure into each trap in the set
  of six,
Paving the way to the new world with salt and sweet.

The poetic method here is one of *taunting* the reader, prodding us at the site of our so-called sensitivity. He isn't content to make us understand our complicity, he wishes to make us feel it: *we* are the executioner's finger; the breast of sugar; the addicted and hyper, ecstatic and doomed ants. In tone as well as content, these stanzas remind us of Aristophanes' aphorism, "The boys kill the frogs in jest. But the frogs die in earnest." Seidel's associative collages routinely drag such apparently disparate things (ants/ Auschwitz/breasts) hallucinatorily together; disparate, yes, but as a late-twenty-first century audience, can we have any doubt that breast fetishism and genocide are somehow connected? It's the abrupt brutality of Seidel's connection-making, and his utter lack of apology, or *cushion* for the ego of his audience, that make him both a poet of nightmare and a poet of humor:

A naked woman my age is a total nightmare.
A woman my age naked is a nightmare.
It doesn't matter. One doesn't care.
One doesn't say it out loud because it's rare
For anyone to be willing to say it,
Because it's the equivalent of buying billboard space to
  display it . . .

Part of the conundrum of Seidel is that he clearly takes personal pleasure in shocking. The adolescence in Seidel's outrageous-ness is obvious. But there is outrage as well as arrogance in the effrontery. And, just when one starts to dismiss the poet as the Savile Row equivalent of a punk rocker, he comes through with something as poignant and naked as the end of "Kill Poem":

The antlered heads are mounted weeping all around the
  walls.

John F. Kennedy is mounted weeping on the wall.
His weeping brother Robert weeps nearby.
Martin Luther King, at bay in Memphis, exhausted, starts to
  cry.
His antlered head is mounted weeping on the wall.
Too much is almost enough, for crying out loud!
Bobby Kennedy announces to a nighttime crowd
That King has died, and then quotes Aeschylus, and then is
  killed.
Kill kill kill kills, appalls,
The American trophies covered in tears that deck the
  American halls.

"There are two ends for Satire—private satisfaction and
public-spiritedness," says the critic A. Melville Clark, and few
poets throw us more consistently into the categorical crisis of
deciding which is operative than Seidel. Yet we *can* tell the difference, whether the speaker is acting as our defender against
power and deceit, our warrior for truth-in-speech, or whether
the speaker is simply being cruel. His daunting set of special effects complicate our judgement as well: his infernal gift for diction, his vividly apocalyptic surrealism, and his unrepentant love
of decadence ride closely alongside a horrified understanding
of our dehumanization.

"Too much is almost enough, for crying out loud": Rage is
what pushes these poems past the limits, through the membrane
of good taste, into the sanctum of the truth. And oddly enough,
Truth is where the laughter begins. Why is the truth so funny?
Because it is so ridiculously hard for us mortals to get there.
Our habit not to know is so strong. As Seidel says earlier in "Kill
Poem," "Our only decision was how to cook the venison."

What is Seidel angry about? Hypocrisy of all brands, dehumanization, the human condition, the American empire,
wealth, race, growing old, modern life, everything, including his
own lifestyle of privilege and detachment. It's the free-handed
dispensation of judgment to himself as well as others, which au-
thenticates this fierce misanthropy.

As a poet, Seidel is a wild, grieving, pissed-off demon. His exclusion from the main camp of American poetry makes a certain sense: demons should be invited into the civic circle only with caution. But Seidel exhibits the shamanic power of humor-rage; it is fearless, and more clear-eyed than most of our poems. The fifteenth century Japanese Zen poet, Ikkyu, explains the cosmic function of a poet like Frederick Seidel, in his poem "Ridiculing Literature":

Humans are endowed with the stupidity of horses and cattle.
Poetry was originally a work out of hell.
Self-pride, false pride, suffering from the passions—
We must sigh for those taking this path
to intimacy with demons.

The Bravery of Trespass

Four Poems about Race by White Poets

Getting off the plane in Newark, New Jersey a few years ago, before the Dodge Poetry Festival, I looked for the car service hired to transport poets to the festival grounds. It turned out I was riding in the same car as Linda Hogan, a Chickasaw Native American poet whom I had not met before.

"Oh, it's nice to meet you," I said. "You and I are on the same panel on Sunday—Poets on Race in Poetry."

Although she and I look pretty much the same—we both could pass for Caucasian Unitarian Minnesotans—she looked at me like I was crazy, and burst into laughter. "What race are *you?*" she said.

Hogan's assumption, one shared by most of us Americans, is that white skin color is disconnected from racial identity. Whiteness is the background against which race happens. "Race" in its common contemporary use, is a word for a (mostly) negatively experienced cultural condition in a dominantly Caucasian society, entailing discrimination on the basis of skin color. In the United States, of course, that assumption is ninety-nine percent true; degrees of brownness have been and continue to be the basis for Dantean social and economic oppression. By comparison, whiteness is historically "unmarked," i.e., is a historically untraumatized state of skin. Or, as the blues musician Big Bill Broonzy, puts it:

> If you's white, you alright,
> If you's brown, stick around,
> But as you's black, oh, brother,
> Get back, get back, get back

Nonetheless, race is the elephant in the living room of American life, and its presence is sensed by all citizens—sometimes acutely, sometimes at a great remove. The fact that race's relevance to their lives is denied by a certain percentage of Americans does not mean it does not press upon their vision. Each time the six o'clock news reports a black man shot in some American street; every time a middle-class citizen locks her car doors while driving through a poor part of town, a little pressure wave of unease ripples through the American psyche, at least on a subliminal level. That shadow, with its complex tension between memory and denial, has been upon the country as long as we have been alive. It is hard to imagine a future free of such shadows will ever exist in this country.

Ironically, as long as race is considered to be the exclusive problem of—and the discursive *property* of—people of color, our situation is perpetuated, unacknowledged, and petrified. As long as *white* is an unremarked-upon color ("What race are *you?*"), we are stuck with the bone in our throat.

In our time, the necessary vocabulary doesn't seem to have been devised that whites can use to name, explore, or describe their own racial discomfort. Speech about race is constrained by the political phobia of saying the wrong thing in the wrong way, a linguistic paranoia that locks us in paralysis. Very little can be said about race in America by a person of "no-color" that is not subject to critique. *Unqualified* to understand the subject, white people are expected to be silent.

One sometimes wonders about such backwardness in the allegedly progressive arts world. Isn't it a form of segregation to always have the Hispanic writer introduced and interviewed by another Hispanic writer, the Asian American writer introduced by the Asian American critic? Aren't the presumptions behind such studied orchestrations of culture mechanical and racist? Isn't it part of our liberated vocation to ignore and shun such sanctions? Isn't it our job as creative writers to speak first and analyze later, to unearth the unspoken, to be reckless? Our great freedom is that we are *not* politicians, nor dissemblers for profit. We don't have to worry about reelection. We are allowed to track the muddy footprints of ambiguity and ambivalence on the living room carpet of propriety. We want to act on behalf of enlightenment, not as self-appointed guardians of fashionable caution.

By way of hopeful testimony, this essay offers four poems by four white American writers who attempt to engage the topic of race in America. Their strategies are wonderfully diverse: oblique, and garrulous, cunning in omission, and sneaky with metaphor, frank with confession, and enigmatic with ambiguity. The variety of their methodologies and what the poems expose about our ongoing awkwardness is rich and resourceful. Most of all, these poems acknowledge race in America as a shared complexity, not the exclusive burden of one group.

I.

Jeffrey McDaniel's poem "What Year Was Heaven Desegregated?" approaches racial reality head-on with a witty bluntness. McDaniel is a gifted metaphorical thinker, and he employs his inventive analogical skills as tongs to handle the charged topic poetically. Here's how his poem begins:

> Watching the news about Diallo, my eight year-old cousin,
>   Jake, asks *why don't they build black people with bulletproof*
>   *skin?* I tell Jake there's another planet, where
>   humans change colors like mood rings.
> You wake up Scottish, and fall asleep Chinese; enter a
>   theater Persian, and exit Puerto Rican. And Earth
> is a junkyard planet, where they send all the broken humans
>   who are stuck in one color.

Dark humor and a science fiction flavor allow the poem a way to comment on this impossibly large subject.[1] McDaniel is also clever in the construct of his rhetorical fiction: a grown-up person explaining the facts of life to a younger one is conventionally allowed to simplify reality through analogies. Just as the younger cousin suggests that bulletproof skin might be helpful

---

1. Amidou Diallo, an unarmed Liberian immigrant, was shot and killed by four New York policemen in 1999.

to African American existence in America, so the older speaker can offer an alternative, Utopian science fiction version of what a "normal" society would look like: "On other planets, you see, . . . humans change colors like mood rings. / You wake up Scottish, and fall asleep Chinese."

In fact, McDaniel's use of poetic fantasy implies that *only* sci-fi logic could account for the world's bizarre history of racial insanity. To approach the topic in the first place requires a certain protective divorce from reality, McDaniel's poem frames racism from such a great distance—from even farther off than the detached distance of whiteness. It makes racism both less real and more real.

In the second section of the poem, the poet brings societal reality much closer through a personal anecdote about his own white "immunity" to persecution. Here the speaker dramatizes his own experience in the system of institutionalized racism:

> Then Jake asks *do they*
> *have ghettoes in the afterlife?* Seven years ago
> I sat in a car, an antenna filled with crack cocaine
>   smoldering
>   between my lips, the smoke spreading
> in my lungs, like the legs of Joseph Stalin's mom in the
>   delivery
>   room. An undercover piglet hoofed up
> to the window. My buddy busted an illegal u-turn, screeched
>   the wrong way down a one-way street.
> I chucked the antenna, shoved the crack rock up my asshole.
>   The cops swooped in from all sides,
> yanked me out. I clutched my ass cheeks like a third fist
>   gripping
>   a winning lotto ticket. The cop yelled
> *white boys only come in this neighborhood for two reasons: to steal*
>   *cars and buy drugs. You already got wheels.*
> I ran into the burning building of my mind. I couldn't see
>   shit.
>   It was filled with crack smoke. I dug
> through the ashes of my conscience, till I found my
>   educated, white
>   male dialect, which I stuck in my voice box
> and pushed play. *Officer, I'm gonna be honest with you Blah,*

51

blah, blah. See, the sad truth is my skin
said everything he needed to know. My skin whispered into
  his pink
    ear *I'm white. You can't pin shit on this*
pale fabric. This pasty cloth is pin resistant. . . .

"What Year Was Heaven Desegregated?" is a poem that narrates a white speaker's confused experience of the racialized world. In its self-scathing intensity, it might be condescendingly consigned to that poetic category called confessional, but its circumstances resonate far beyond a speaker's singular experience. Every possessor of white skin's privilege, says McDaniel's speaker, is a sinner, one who enjoys the leisure of unearned advantage.

The speaker recognizes that he is entangled in a collective injustice, and is a beneficiary of racial imbalance. The speaker's guilt is not just channeled into middle-class self-contempt, but projected into a fierce contempt for the whole system, the system in which white boys walk, and black ones are locked up. McDaniel's surrealist, mechanical imagery ("I found my educated, white / male dialect, which I stuck in my voice box") extends the alien imagery established earlier in the poem, of a "robot world" where human beings on automatic pilot are helplessly enmeshed in a broken system. The speaker, though white, is not insensible to the hellish split in American consciousness.

McDaniel's poem exhibits nerve in taking on the difficult subject with a skillful blend of worldly truth and imaginative adventure. His use of fantasy leavens, but does not whitewash the factual realism which is also part of the poem. This poet's way of handling this topic—a topic that most white poets simply avoid—is ingenious, substantial, and bold.

II.

The strategy of Lucia Perillo's poem, "The Wolves of Illinois," is more ambiguous and glancing in its treatment of whiteness and race. In Perillo's poem, the contact between black and white Americans is not frontal, dramatic, nor especially commented upon; but peripheral, uncomfortable, and inarticulate. The situation is simple: at a nature sanctuary, members of two races find themselves alongside each other, seeking a glimpse of wild life. What the reader gets is a view of another kind of creature—the complex, under-articulated wildness of everyday race relations. Here's how Perillo's poem begins:

> When I stopped along the road and climbed the platform
> that thewildlife people built, I saw the dead grass moving.
> A darker gold that broke free from the pale gold of the
> field.

> "Wolves," said the man who stood beside me on the
> platform. On hisother side stood his wife and children, I
> assumed, dressed as if they'dcome from church.

> a boy and girl, her scalp crosshatched with partings from her
> braids.Note that this is my way of announcing they were
> black

> or African American, I am shy not only of the terminology
> but of the subject altogether

In Perillo's poem the drama of racial estrangement is projected, in part, onto the absence of adequate language—"What do I call this?" wonders Perillo's speaker, narrating her story to the reader. "Is the word *black* or *African American?* Is it *coyote* or *wolf?*" Having to choose between different names for things becomes emblematic of the incomprehensible and perhaps uncrossable breach between brown and white:

> and my being torn about the language makes me nervous
> from the start. "Look at the wolves," he told his
> children . . .

> "Those are coyotes," I said . . .

> > Because I know the wolves were coyotes;

> *the wolves were coyotes*

> and so I said "There are no wolves in Illinois."

"I am shy not only of the terminology but of the subject altogether," says Perillo's honest speaker, "and my being torn about language makes me nervous from the start."

The contest to be right about the identity of wildlife is the superficial conflict of the scene, but what becomes eloquent is not who wins, but the skirmishing, indirect, inarticulate style in which the two protagonists struggle: never facing each other, nor allowing their disagreement to escalate. Each strives to be an "authority," but the buried dimensions of the struggle—personal pride, dignity, competitiveness, and American history—represent race relations in our time. Agreement seems impossible, concession is unacceptable, and direct contact is best avoided.

"Check out the wolves," he said (the minutes ticking)
(the minutes nuzzling each other's flanks)

The scene captures the fragility and uneasiness that members of one race feel for another. Symbolically, the situation also implies that the two people actually see two different *realities*. Some literary critic might evasively say that "The Wolves of Illinois," is about *language*, but in fact it is about estrangement, separation, difference, and the inchoate burden of the American slavery legacy, though none of that is overtly named. Race is only an incidental smudge in the narrative, but that irritating, ominous, and profound smudge affects everything else. Its incomplete, uninspected, unarticulated subject matter mirrors the way that race is a peripheral, disturbing presence in the ongoing order of our days.

III.

Lydia Davis is well-known as a writer of short, obliquely-angled fictions, but Davis frequently uses techniques that make it quite reasonable to consider her a poet. Her one-and-one-half-page piece called "The Family," employs the sterilized factual tone of a police report. Writing in a flat, utterly objective voice with no inflection or accompanying commentary, Davis describes interactions observed between a number of characters in a public park:

(1) Fat young white woman pulls white baby by one arm onto quilt spread on grass. (2) Little black boy struggles with older black girl over swing, (3) is ordered to sit down on grass, (4) stands sullen while (5) fat white woman heaves to her feet, walks to him, and smacks him. (6) Little black boy whimpers, lies on his back on grass while (7) fat white woman plays with baby and (8) young black man orders black girl off swing. (9) Young black man begins wrestling in play with long-haired white girl who (10) protests while (11) tall, bony, wrinkled, mustachioed white man in baseball cap stands with arms crossed, back hunched, walkie-talkie attached to right hip and (12) back girl lies down with face in baby's face. (13) Baby peers up and around black girl when (14) white girl protests more loudly as (15) young black man slaps her buttocks and (16) older white man watches with arms crossed. (17) White girl breaks free of young black man and runs toward river crying as (18) young black man runs easily after her and (19) older white man in baseball cap runs awkwardly after her, one hand on walkie-talkie at his hip. (20) Young black man picks up white girl and carries her back . . .

"The Family" places the reader in a state of uncertainty about these events and their meanings. What does it *mean* that the characters are of different races? Do our narrative stereotypes and anxieties *help* us interpret what is going on, or do they distort our perception? Will the older white man produce a gun and use it in some violent defense of white rights? Is that white girl being harassed by that young black man?

The description of the "plot," and the lack of interpretation on the part of the narrator provokes the reader to draw culturally conditioned conclusions—to impose various narratives on the events. Davis's stripped-down story elicits and showcases the stereotyped notions we bring to our everyday perception. Like the Rorschach blot test administered as part of a psychological assessment, Davis profiles the reader's conditioned projection of American racial assumptions. What is going on?

As it turns out, nothing bad comes to pass. It is simply "one family" on an outing, and our confusion arises from the mixture of the characters' races and ages, their relations. At the end of the narrative, the family packs up and goes home, as peaceful and disorganized as any family on a picnic:

(34) White woman returns with black man and bends to gather quilt and bag from grass. (35) White man in baseball cap holds small sleeping bag open while (36) young white woman puts baby in. (37) Young white woman orders black boy up off ground. (38) Black boy shakes head and stays on ground . . . (42) older white man follows, holding crying black boy by hand. (43) Family leaves playground and enters dusty road. (44) Family stops to wait for white man in baseball cap, who (45) returns slowly to park, picks up pair of child's thongs from grass, and (46) rejoins family. (47) Family walks on, heading toward marsh, short bridge, and red sky.

In her ominous, deadpan and quiet style, Davis's piece does one job of literature: it pressures us to fill in the blanks and feel what is there to feel. Her enigmatic orchestration threatens us with the imaginative potential of racial complication. That the trouble never arrives is a strange relief. And yet the American potential for violence and misunderstanding hovers around the scene atmospherically, and for the duration of our reading, we have felt that familiar curse.

IV.

Doug (also known as Diana) Goetsch's narrative-meditative poem, "Black People Can't Swim" offers the most positive portrait of racial coexistence of the four poems here.

In Goetsch's narrative scene, the white male speaker is hanging out with a group of African-American women; he is curious, garrulous, ignorant, and undefensive. The specific gift that Goetsch's poem brings us is the representation of our true, deep racial curiosity—the characters are neither frightened nor traumatized, neither angry, wary, or self-conscious. Goetsch's speaker's guileless curiosity is charming. This, perhaps—the good faith of curiosity—may be the most healing asset Americans possess, and it constitutes our best argument for hopefulness. Merely to model, foster and accommodate that curiosity, as this poem does, is a worthy poetic function. Here's how the poem starts:

When I told Patricia how much I loved the pool at the Y,
she said, "Oh, black people can't swim,"
which made me grateful to be let in on this,
not the information, but the intimacy—
the fact that she could let fly with such a piece
of black-on-black attitude without the slightest
bit of shame or self-consciousness. We were in
a restaurant, me and five black women . . .
                                    who were paying
more attention than any white females I'd ever seen
to a football game on the high-definition TV.

Goetsch, like the other writers featured here, is a canny rheto-
rician, who must steer his unusual narrative through the treach-
erous politicized waters of objectification and "exoticizing the
other." One smart choice he makes is to deliver his anecdote
in dialogue form—as a consequence, most of the perspective
upon women of color is delivered, not as the speaker's observations, but as reported speech, as the testimony of an "inside
informant." What is more, the speaker greets his informants'
revelations about the lives of African American women with an
attitude of delight and wonder—his education is progressing.

That doesn't mean the speaker renders himself invisible, in
the manner of the narrator of Davis's poem, "The Family." Here,
the white speaker augments his narrative with authorial asides—
"which made me / grateful to be in on this" and "We were all
toddlers when Martin dreamed / of little black children and
little white children / going to school arm in arm. He dreamed
this too: / a restaurant table where we were free to reveal / not
just our true, but our mysterious, irrational selves / in the presence of the other tribe without apology."

Later in "Black People Can't Swim," the speaker asks about
being escorted into a store by one of his African-American woman friends.

    Earlier, on the walk over, she pulled me
away from the group into a leather shop
to show me a $200 Italian bag on layaway.
"And what did you say?"
"Nice bag."

"That's not what she wanted to hear."
"Which was?"
They eyed each other, deciding who would tell.
"Honey, when a sister shows a man something
on layaway she wants him to buy it."
"No way—" but they were all nodding, and I had to
love this country, or this ten square feet of it,
where they could tell me about men and women
and race and layaway.

Goetsch's upbeat narrative depicts at least one small parcel of American terrain—"ten square feet"—in which MLK's dream is being realized, in increments. The ignorance of one race about another, in this scenario, can be relieved by frankness and friendship. It's a moment of good news, and it presents a counterpoint to the dark vision recorded in McDaniel's poem, and the irresolvable, helpless friction portrayed in Perillo's poem.

Of course, one can imagine a critic faulting Goetsch's poem for its sentimentality, or its stereotyping, or for its "appropriation" of black voices by a white narrator, or even for his speaker's liberal passivity.

In fact, any of these four poems by white people about the topic of race could be faulted or disqualified for some sort of near-sightedness, over-simplification, or historical omission. But one might as well accuse empathy itself of being a presumptuous act of the imagination. To assume is not always an act of arrogant blindness—it can also be an act of hope and courage, from which fresh possibilities arise.

It is worth our while to admire the range of these poetic tableaux, to appreciate the diversity of conceptual risks and technical skills employed to make each of these poems work on its own terms. In the world of a million stories, and a million standing places, no perspective has a monopoly. Different actualities coexist; what is true hides in some layered composite of all of them.

Each of these narratives displays a white speaker struggling to be aware of whiteness as a color with consequences, and to comprehend race as a reality in which he or she is clearly one element. Likewise, these poems individually recognize the presence of whiteness as an inconvenience, and sometimes as a kind of injustice for others.

They trouble the questions that many black and brown and yellow writers, and women thinkers have asked in the past, "Who owns the terms? How can I find a way to converse with other viewpoints without using the terminology and discourse invented by those others? Do I *want* to have the discussion and will I be permitted to say how the truth is for me?"

Our dialogue about race is complex, unresolved, and will probably be endless; a thing to be enacted forever on our shaky, shattered, and traumatized national ground. It requires of us a belief in the willingness of others, and a trust that even our misunderstandings will not be intentionally misunderstood.

No Laughing Matter
Race, Poetry, and Humor

At a 2011 National Book Award (NBA) event, in the half-full auditorium of the New School in New York City, commemorative of the NBA's fiftieth anniversary, a panel met to discuss, in public, the aesthetic "track record" of the NBA poetry awards. The panel included Susan Stewart, James Longenbach, Stephen Burt, Elizabeth Alexander, myself, and Maureen McClane.

In some ways this event was an occasion of justified self-celebration—over fifty years, a surprising number of groundbreaking collections of American poetry have been selected by the NBA; choices that represent the insight and sometimes even the daring of past NBA committees. Past winners have included such unpredictable and groundbreaking texts as Adrienne Rich's *Diving into the Wreck*, Robert Bly's *The Light Around the Body*, as well as collections by William Bronk and Lucille Clifton—none of them by any means pro forma candidates for establishment approval—but special, perhaps even crucial books in the pilgrim's progress of American poetry.

But it was the first speaker of the night whose remarks were perhaps definitive for how they set in place a template that could not be forgotten.

Elizabeth Alexander opened her remarks with a rueful and witty preface: "Apparently," she remarked, "I have been put on earth to count colored heads; when they are there and when they are not. It is tiresome sometimes, but it is a habit which is in fact an ethical practice—count and name; mark absence; herald presence; speak silence."

It was a droll yet serious beginning, self-consciously wry about the unenviable duty of monitoring racial equity in culture. Alexander went on to observe the disproportionately large number of white males in the NBA roll books, and the comparatively very few women and minorities represented.

"In looking through the list we were given to consider tonight [of past winners of the NBA], the headline for my five minutes was clear; there were no black winners of the National Book Award in poetry from 1950 until 1999. Numbers don't lie. No Latino winners, no women . . . two black women, two black men, in fifty years."

"No Gwendolyn Brooks," Alexander continued. "No Robert Hayden; no Amiri Baraka; no Jay Wright. No Michael Harper. No Yusef Komunyaaka. No Rita Dove." Now Alexander's tone seemed less wry and more aggrieved, as she recited what seemed to be a list of injustices. "I wish," said Alexander, "that poetry were much different than the Oscars when it comes to how cultural capital is doled out to people of color. Cultural capital is real. In the conferring of materiality and meaning, who gets the gold sticker matters. It matters. Who gets the prizes matters."

Then—in a bold move, considering the occasion—Alexander told an unpleasant, perhaps damning anecdote from the annals of the past, drawn from a biography of Wallace Stevens.[1] It happened in 1952, during a meeting of the NBA poetry judges. While waiting for a tardy member to arrive, the committee, which included Stevens, passed the time by looking at photographs of previous committees. Stevens, on seeing a photo in which Gwendolyn Brooks appeared, remarked, "Who's the coon?"

What *was* the motive—and what was the effect—of Alexander's choice to publicly remind panelists and audience of the not-so distant, not-so-pretty past? Stevens' racism is well-known, if not frequently mentioned, and it is a fact which complicates, if not the stature of his poems, at least the canonization of the person who made them. Like American racism at large, such complicating facts should not be swept under the rug. Indisputably, someone must keep pulling back the curtain on the historical backstage. And, of course, our collective historical memory, our hauntedness, is one ongoing source of our humanity, of our often-inadequate attempts to improve ourselves. Some memo-

---

1. Wallace Stevens, *A Biography: The Later Years*, by Joan Richardson.

ries must be reawakened. Or, as one of Michael Harper's best-known poems says, "In nightmare begins responsibility."

Compared to Stevens' recorded remark, Alexander's talk was a model of diplomatic gentility. Nonetheless, Alexander's speech unmistakably was aimed at "outing" Stevens; and by proxy, "outing" the National Book Award as an institution with a racist history.

There is nothing particularly unusual about this episode of contemporary literary culture. In fact, the proceedings of the evening offer an opportunity for insight *because* of their cultural familiarity. From such episodes, in fact, we can measure our status quo on the race spectrometer. First, we can observe that it is as difficult as ever not to take matters of race and privilege personally. Secondly, we can see that nothing marks the conversation about race more than humorlessness and compulsion. These compulsions are structured by and laden with subtexts that are only half-visible.

Compulsion is a strong word choice when it comes to describing the conversation of American race, but how can we avoid it? Just as American racial scenarios often have a furtive, surreal, dreamlike quality (the shooting of Trayvon Martin, for example)— so our speech displays the agency of unconscious motives in our choices, tone, and behavior. In matters of race, subterranean forces always seem to be actively coexistent with those explicable by rationality.

White writers, for their part, are caught in the double- or triple-bind of power, apology, and hazard. As a result, they feel mostly compelled to say *nothing*, at least nothing remotely controversial, that is, on the subject of race and aesthetics. White literary approbation, or disagreement, is registered in silence. On the evening in question, the white poets performed their roles in the customary manner: gazing abstractedly into space as Alexander spoke, or smiling with liberal sheepishness and nodding in agreement. Yet there is something so passive in this white performance as to be unsatisfying. At most, the silent acquiescence seems to signify, "I *might* agree with you," or "For reasons I don't want to articulate, I consent to be powerless, i.e., remain silent, in this conversation."

Alexander felt compelled, that evening, to remind the community at large about the formative racism of our past. This arduous but important responsibility! How important and valuable it is that a self-elected, gutsy individual (not an institution) gallantly perform that role for the community. As Alexander's preface acknowledged, "Tonight, I shall be the Watchkeeper of Memory."

As for subtexts, one subtext pretty much shared by both non-white and liberal white persons in the American zeitgeist, is that the historical oppressor must be transformed into a penitent before equity can be achieved. Compensation, if not economic, then at least psychological, must be offered. A humbling—like the one Alexander administered to Stevens and the NBA—must be ritually enacted as a form of reparations. As a corollary, the increased elevation of the historically victimized class is another kind of ritual equity. As Alexander said, emphatically, "Prizes matter—they *matter*." Her message is clear: more prizes need to be given to writers of color.

Such subtexts underlie our racial conversations at every level, from the very political and very public to the very private. "What is it our responsibility to say?" we ask ourselves. Then, "What do we *really* think and feel?" Then, "What are we *allowed* to say?" Where do truth, courtesy, frankness, aesthetics, history, and justice coexist, and where do they contradict or interfere with each other? For, after all, our racial stories and our psychic fabrications around race are as layered as the long narrative of our individual bodies; as private and complex as our family stories.

The subtexts of American literary whiteness include the whole long shadow of American racial history; first, of slavery, and secondly, of ongoing economic and social inequality—though to say it in these abstract terms feels like a diminishment of the vast American tragedy. We stand indefinitely, and anxiously, we are soaked and poisoned, in those shadows.

Another part of the shadow is ongoing white privilege, and the natural instinct to retain advantage. Take me as an example, though anyone else on that panel would serve as well. On the one hand, I'll acknowledge my privilege readily; on the other hand, I hope not to be inconvenienced. Secretly too, my ego will privately continue to believe that whatever success I have experienced has been legitimate, is deserved, not a product of my whiteness; that it has been earned by my individual talent and hard work.

These are called *subtexts* for a reason; I would not express such feelings and beliefs casually in public because of the hazard that accompanies public frankness on the topic of race. The topic itself, everyone knows, has become the territorial property of persons of color. Thus, the frank, exploratory, spontaneous speech that our shared reality requires can easily end in blame, anger, or disgrace. Thus I won't ever disagree, openly, with the consensual liberal parameters of the racial conversation. I will be a yes-person. Occasionally, in a marginal way, among my liberal white friends, I will ironically acknowledge that the machinery of affirmative action is at work in the cultureplace. This calculation of equity (counting heads) is the price of repairing history. I consent to that machinery—and, though I would *personally* prefer not to pay the disadvantageous price of it—oh well, it's not about me.

My main public obligation, you understand, is to appear composed and collected. Whether I feel clear-headed or good about it or not, to be conflicted about race in public would, in itself, be an admission of confusion about these labyrinthine American matters. And confusion is now itself suspect.

The gap between these two unconscious positions—the position of historical plaintiff, played that evening by Alexander, and the position of uneasy but affluent possessors of privilege, played by myself and others—is substantial, and, so far, mostly unbridged. Both positions seem petrified and fossilized. Our consensual silence—the particular silence of white liberals—on the subject of race is paradoxically, ultimately an obstacle to acknowledging the present and moving into the future. It's not hard to see that we—both white and black poets—are still breathing through straws.

Brothers and sisters—(am I even allowed to say that?)—we are haunted.

One of my questions is: can a conscious poetry help bridge it?

Humor

It is too bad that our collective superego, our consciousness of tragedy and history, demands our utter seriousness on this subject. Because humor is, in all of our affairs, a way to let the cats and the dogs out of the bag. Humor makes the ugly bearable, and the truth audible. Humor releases resentments, truth, misunderstanding, and our relief simultaneously. It also embodies our ambivalences and our contradictory understandings. In a way, in fact, our ability to joke is some basic testament of freedom.

Here's the poet Paul Beatty, from the preface to his novel, *The White Boy Shuffle*:

> In the quest for equality, black folks have tried everything. We've begged, revolted, entertained, intermarried, and are still treated like shit. Nothing works, so why suffer the slow deaths of toxic addiction and the American work ethic when the immediate gratification of suicide awaits? In glorious defiance of the survival instinct, Negroes stream into Hillside, California, like lemmings. Every day they wishfully look heavenward, peering into the California smog for a metallic gray atomic dot that will gradually expand until it explodes some one thousand feet over our natural and processed heads. It will be the Emancipation Disintegration. Lunch counters, bus seats, and executive washrooms be damned; our mass suicide will be the ultimate sit-in.

Paul Beatty is still my favorite poet—brown, yellow, or white—of American race. Even though he does not write poetry anymore—he is now a prizewinning novelist—his two books of poems describe the gamesmanship, insanity, and suffering of race with an acrobatic freedom I have found in no one else's work. No one comes close to passages like this from "About the Author":

> me and angry sister x
> would read our poems over breakfast
> they were fresh
> smelt of incense and just crushed hummus

garbanzo beans are the seeds of freedom
i couldn't wait till my dreads tickled the tips of my ears

we figured going to hear this established poet
might promote our hair growth

a poet whose description under his picture read

the author is a demolitions expert an accomplished
    marksman philosopher
black belt voodoo witch doctor lobbyist who lives in a thatch
    hut in rwanda
and is at present trying to get congress to pass the james
    bond act
law that permits black people to drink martinis with a
    straight face
and to kill white folks with impunity . . .

we sat and listened in a white church

but this poet had on a pressed starched collared shirt . . .

he was missing
his mutton chop hate whitey side burns
and read long monotone poems . . .

after we left we realized he never said black   not once
                    maybe we'd missed something . . .

who turned the magic fire hose on his dashiki
and turned it into one of them
irish spring soap commercial prep school sweaters . . .

fuck the elephant's graveyard
i want to know where does the revolutionary spirit go to die

Beatty has sardonic fun, and he *makes* fun even against a context of considerable sorrow. In particular, Beatty's poetic genius is how adroitly he plays with clashing layers of idiom and stereotype which cross-fertilize and cross-examine both sides of the street, whiteness and blackness. He makes fun of the myth of equal opportunity and the fact of social liability, of over-compensating white guilt, and fantasizing welfare moms. He ventriloquizes both white- and black-inflected speech.

Why do I find his work so reassuring? Because, for all its wild tones (empathy, anger, corrosive sarcasm), the poems in *Joker, Joker, Deuce* are neither overly idealistic nor especially complaining. Beatty really is not promoting anything but the comedic carnival of realism. Vast injustices of tragic proportions are part of that carnival. To me, there's more truth, reality, insight, and dark acrobatic freedom about race in Beatty's work than in a slew of sincere collections of poetry that take on the subject. And freedom of speech is a marvelous kind of freedom.

Thomas Sayers Ellis is another young poet who fights the historical race battle with humorous fists. In his recent book, *Skin, Ink*. Ellis has a section called *Society for the Friends of Former Property*. Ellis's funny is a grim-funny, but its tone illustrates a kind of "coming out," emotionally refreshing because it seems more real than the sanctimony and reverence of much other work. Here is a passage from Ellis's poem "The Obama Hour":

> Finally one of us is properly
> positioned to run. By "us" I mean Black,
> by "positioned" I mean White
> and by "run" I mean Race and its varied speeds of
>   darkness . . .
> including the difficult qualifying times
> between the theft of our arrival and all hate crimes.

The twisty compressions of a passage like this create a greater-than-usual intimacy between the writer and readers, either white or black, through their frankness—frank aggression and playful anger. Ellis's sincere jabbing is compactly thoughtful and verbally adroit in the way that humor is swift. It makes fun of the explanations it skips over and reformulates history as a mode of discussing it ("by 'run' I mean Race and its varied speeds of darkness"). Elsewhere, in the poem "No Easy Task," Ellis's speaker says, "The problem / with American poetry / is there's not enough Africa / in it; bling-bling has more / rhythm and imagery / than all of Ashbery."

Moving at this speed, the speed of jabbing humor, one might

get *somewhere* in the racial dialogue, somewhere beyond redundant reprisals of the historical positions; speeches assuming the politically correct postures of our time, one more time.

What humor brings into the racial conversation is flexibility and resilience, the freedom to play against codes, rather than be imprisoned by categories. Laughter directed at the self, as well as the other, at the unsaid as well as the unsayable, is a freedom that releases the pressures of identity, and maybe even points the way to revelation. In humor, boundaries are loosened, not fortified. This is a lot to ask from individuals and groups who have been punished by category (poets of color)—and likewise of other people who have been *protected* by category (uncolored poets)—and yet, such self-exposé is what is needed, and such linguistic-psychological performances are something which poetry is uniquely well-suited to deliver.

What White Poets Haven't Done

If African-American poets, generationally, are beginning to write over the lines and into the cracks of racial self-protectionism, white poets have not really stepped up to the same challenge. Poetry by white poets is largely barricaded into a kind of ivory tower of niceness, or a cul de sac of political correctness. Most often, the poems of white writers simply practice omission. White poets—always sincere, always politically correct, often perceptive—are largely petrified when it comes to working creatively with the more fictitious, performative aspects of race. I don't know many poems about race by white poets that are not boring, which is to say they repeat the predigested social stances we have been trained to declare.

The cautiousness—and muteness—of white poets on American race is understandable, even appropriate. Because of our history of unshared power, racial humor in white mouths is legitimately suspect. It is easy for a white writer to get it wrong, to thoughtlessly evoke the history of oppression just by opening his mouth. It is one thing for Chris Rock to make a joke about watermelon; it would be another thing for a white comedian. We could say that the price-tag is still on that joke—and that black

Americans have already bought and paid for it. A haunted sea of grief underlies Billie Holiday's singing "Strange Fruit"—but the song becomes something different sung by Diana Krall.

Nonetheless, race is such a huge presence in American life; we are saturated in its tensions and confusions, guilts, resentments and hallucinations, its curiosities and passions—it is finally, artistically and politically, unavoidable. Inevitable, too, that we shall make progress in our permissiveness to speak, our efforts to deploy art's powers towards the thawing of traumatized, frightened, and self-protective discourse. The poems of grievance and testimony written by poets of color will become tiresome unless they innovate their own consciousness. "Identity poetics," says Reginald Shepherd, "is *boring*, giving back the already known, in an endless and endlessly self-righteous confirmation of things as they are. . . . [but] The greatest literature has always engaged in the generation of new realities, not the reiteration of the same old given reality." And it is time for white poets to interrogate and publicly explore our own layered consciousness in walking around in a world colored by the history of color. It is time for grace, daring, and courage in the presence of the other, in the interests of open discourse.

Until white writers are as open and frank and funny about their own anxieties, blindnesses, and feelings about race—whiteness and brownness—as black poets and comedians are now, until those imaginary poems of the future are written; stiffness, reserve, suspicion, and jealousy, formality and distrust and silence—not equity—will be the ghost in the room in our communities and our art. Fortunately, not just our hauntedness, but our powerful mutual curiosity about race litigates in favor of openness.

The Models of Fiction and Theatre

I wonder why poetry has largely lagged behind other literary art forms. American theatre and fiction, for example, flourish in comical, transgressive, and ultimately—we hope—healing treatments of race. August Wilson, Spike Lee, and the 2011 play *Clybourne Park* by Bruce Norris explore the confused backstages of racial correctness. America's readiness for humor about race is signified by the roster of superstar multiracial comedians. The comedian W. Kamau Bell does his part, not just through comedy but economics; he has a "bring a friend of a different race" two-for-one night at his performances. The comedians Key and Peele are brilliant chameleon shapeshifters in their racial comedies.

American fiction writers have also allowed themselves more liberty in writing about race—Edward Jones, Jonathan Lethem, Colson Whitehead, and others have creatively spin-doctored the sociology of racism. The main character of Mat Johnson's graphic novel *Incognegro* is a light skinned black man who goes undercover, infiltrates, and then exposes groups of Ku Klux Klansmen in the South. *Incognegro* combines elements of pulp noir literature, of comic books, and of adventure writing. There's something at once serious and untraumatized about the cultural engagement in this novel, and the resilience with which stereotypes are rendered shows a faith in the progressiveness of perception.

But poetry and poets—are they doomed to be categorically sincere, and therefore conservative? It seems that too much solemnity or fearfulness has imparted something stiff and dutiful to how white poets handle race. Poetry's attachment to sincerity, its self-inflicted obligation to be eternally sensitive may have the unintentional effect of retarding the potential in our craft for complexity and danger.

Return to the Scene

Meanwhile, back at the NBA auditorium, later that same evening, another memorable, racially-contorted interchange occurred. Stephen Burt had just praised Terrance Hayes's new collection, *Lighthead*—which had been awarded the 2010 National Book Award—as an exceptional book which unified and represented the best in American poetics of our moment. Burt, a white poet, naturally did not mention—though it was implicit—the fact that the book was written by an African-American poet. Burt's *subtext*, of course, was that this book, *Lighthead*, and its recognition should satisfy both the high aesthetic tradition of the National Book Award audience, and the desire, expressed by Alexander, for more equitable racial distribution of cultural recognition.

In the Q and A that followed, an elderly lady in the audience raised her skinny pale arm and asked, "Why didn't Major Jackson [like Hayes, a youngish African-American male poet] win the award," she asked, "instead of Terrance Hayes?"

Uh-oh. It was a poignant, awkward, and deeply discouraging moment. For, after all, the lady's unconscious assumption—that one black poet was as good as another when it came to prize-winning—confirmed our worst suspicions about categorical imperatives, about the blindness to individuality fostered by racialized vision.

If any doubt existed about the veracity of Alexander's critique—about arrested development of perception at the cultural level—that point was made.

Yet the moment also represented the aesthetic myopia that comes from head-counting. After all, Alexander and the lady from Dubuque *both* were counting heads of color. "Numbers don't lie." "Awards matter." But, in fact, numbers *can* lie. It is worth noting that Alexander fielded the woman's question with grace and kindness.

Add one more episode. The next night, as a counterpart to the panel discussion of NBA history by talking heads, a brief poetry reading was held elsewhere in the city. The six poet-critics of the NBA poetry panel discussion were each invited to read a poem of their own, and a poem by one of the NBA Poetry Prize winners of the past. Five poets read work that evening, and of the five, two chose to read poems by Wallace Stevens. Maybe it is mere speculation about what compulsions and subtextual motives underlay their selections, but it seems quite possible that the readers who chose Stevens poems were marshaling a kind of defense of Stevens—not of the man, but the poetry—in response to Alexander's attack of the night before.

White apologetic liberalism only gets us so far. Nor do, appearances suggest, finger-wagging demands for cultural reparations have a great record of success. The poem confessing complicity, playing the violin of historical guilt; the poem which asserts solidarity with the oppressed, in a ringing tone of self-righteousness—how often these can seem like hollow gestures.

In an ironic way, the sophistication and familiarity of our discourse about race has made us less able to speak authentically; our public conversation has made us as polite and clumsy as people playing catch while wearing oven mittens. What we get, repeatedly, is the stilted performance of Reparations, as opposed to the Conversation about Literary Racial Reality.

We would like for the narrative to end with justice, but for the time being, that outcome seems unlikely. It might be better to aim for Mercy, the level playing field of Forgiveness or at least, greater courage and honesty. The humility that comes from self-knowledge and the acceptance of our imperfect, tragic, mutually-entangled circumstances—that is the place where we must stand. In our ignorant, denying, confounded, decade-after-decade grapplings with race, our ignorance has to be out in the open, visible to both white and black speakers, to offer any hope of progress.

Say you have a dream and in that dream you have a broken arm. You are driving around a strange city looking for first aid. It is late at night in the dream, and raining. Block after block you drive, through intersections, past warehouses and gymnasiums. You go through township after township. The neon glow of tilted pink martini glasses, the fluorescent glare of all-night garages, and shopping malls with their acres of empty parking lot—you keep going. You have seen several signs saying *Mercy Clinic, Mercy Emergency Care, Mercy Pharmacy*, but you keep on going. Your arm hurts. A hospital is what you need, but you are looking for the one you've heard about, the one called *Justice*. That's the situation all of us are in.

"I Seem to Be at a Great Feast"

The War Poems of Guillaume Apollinaire

When the poet Guillaume Apollinaire enlisted in the French artillery in December of 1914, his friends received the news with deep dismay. Apollinaire was a pivotal orchestrator of the roiling Paris art scene, a scene that included Picasso, de Chirico, Max Jacob, and Henri Rousseau. Through his tireless literary entrepreneurship and his flashy, opinionated art criticism, Apollinaire had made himself the foremost advocate of the new spirit in literature and painting. His career, along with theirs, was coming to a boil. Past the age of conscription, he was thirty-five, not even legally a French citizen[1] (his mother's nationality was Polish-Russian), Apollinaire was in no danger from the draft. Moreover, he had practiced the café life of a freelance intellectual for years, part of an artistic cadre for whom borderline irresponsibility was an aesthetic principle. Apollinaire seemed an unlikely candidate for following orders, not to mention the hardship and violence of war. His battles were aesthetic, his weapons were his tongue and pen.

But for Apollinaire, a soldier's life was a revelation. He loved his training in arms and horseback riding, learning to use and care for the famous French 75 cannon. He delighted in the discovery of his physical prowess, his ability to keep up with men fifteen years younger than he, the manly camaraderie of barracks life, the welter of new sights and sounds and information. "Soldiering is my true profession," he wrote his Parisian friends. To another he wrote, from training camp, "I love art

---

1. One motive for Apollinaire's enlistment, in addition to adventure, might have been to attain French citizenship in exchange for his service.

so much, I have joined the artillery." And because waiting and idleness turned out to be a part of life in uniform, he wrote a great deal—"enough," said one of his correspondents, "to kill the postman." Between December l914 and March 1916, in the thirty-eighth regiment of field artillery, at times using an ink-well made from a cartridge casing, Apollinaire produced a passionate, strangely-uncelebrated body of poetry. Still compelling and eerily effervescent, they challenge our modern assumptions about art and war.

> The sky is starred by the Boche's shells
> The marvelous forest where I live is giving a ball
> The machine gun plays a tune in three-fourths time
> But have you the word
>   Eh! yes the fatal word
> To the loopholes To the loopholes Leave the picks there
>
> Like a lost star searching for its seasons
> Heart exploded shell you whistled your love song
> And your thousand suns have emptied the caissons
> That the gods of my eyes fill silently
>
> We love you oh life and we get on your nerves . . .
>
>   Hear our shells sing
> Their deep-purple love hailed by our men going to die
>
> The wet springtime the night light the attack
>
> It's raining my soul it's raining but it's raining dead eyes
>
> Ulysses how many days to get back to Ithaca
>
> Lie down in the straw and dream a fine remorse
> Which as a pure effect of art is aphrodisiac
>   ("April Night 1915")

The speed, the range of association and of register are still astonishing: "It's raining my soul it's raining but it's raining dead eyes / Ulysses how many days to get back to Ithaca?"

Apollinaire's war poems are startling for their enthusiasm. Irony and melancholy are not *absent* from their rich tonal palette, but more often the speaker sounds like a large schoolboy allowed to stay out late, delighted with the glamour of his toys. The poems rejoice in the spectacle, the improbability and the technological glory of modern warfare. A year before, in his 1913 poem "Zone," he had compared Christ to an aviator "who holds the world record for altitude." In the war poems of *Calligrammes*, translated by Anne Hyde Greet, notes of sobriety are sounded, but the prevailing mood is one of rhapsodic, intoxicated excitement. "The Little Car," his poem about the outbreak of hostilities, portrays his sense of historical adventure, and even, of destiny:

> August 31, 1914
> A little before midnight I left Deauville
> In Rouveyre's little car
>
> Counting the chauffeur we were three
>
> We said farewell to a whole era
> Furious giants were rising over Europe
> Eagles flew from their eyrie to wait for the sun
> Voracious fish ascended from abysses
> Nations hurled together so they might learn to know one
>   another . . .
>
> I felt within me skillful new beings
> Build and even arrange a new universe
> A merchant with unheard-of wealth and whose size was
>   prodigious
> Arranged an extraordinary showcase

"Nations hurled together so they might learn to know one another"—Apollinaire's definition of war as a terrible blind date is comic, cosmic, and, on one level, terribly true. Apollinaire's uncensored gusto for the conflict, so controversial on the surface, sprang in part from his unquenchable thirst for modernity. Even in the maw of World War I, the cataclysm which would destroy humanist faith for most of Europe, Apollinaire believes in progress, both material and cosmic. He is happy to say goodbye to the old era because of his confidence that the next era will be marvelous, "an extraordinary showcase." And it was part of his heroic subjectivity to feel that his own fate and that of the century were intimately entwined. "The Little Car" concludes:

We arrived in Paris
Just as they were posting the draft
We realized my friend and I
That the little car had driven us into a New era
And although we were both already mature men
We had just been born

Apollinaire was one of the first truly twentieth-century poets. Like his friends the first-generation Cubist painters, he broke rules with abandon—his demolition of conventions and his consequent discoveries prefigured most of what has passed for avant-garde ever since. One of his many innovations was the removal of all punctuation from his book *Alcools*, in 1913, an impulsive act undertaken the night before the poems went to press. Goodbye, boundaries! The relationship between beginnings, endings, and middles, between poetic fragments and poetic wholes, might be said to have changed that night. In the war poems, the lack of grammatical boundary seems expressive of confusion, excitement, and a kind of circumstantial collective consciousness:

The soldiers are coming
The village is almost asleep in the perfumed light
A priest wears a helmet
A bottle of champagne is artillery yes or no
Vine stocks like ermine on a coat of arms
Hello soldiers
I see them running to and fro
Hello soldiers you bottles of champagne in which the blood
    ferments
                            ("The Vine Grower of Champagne")

Often enough, thrill and horror intermingle in Apollinaire's war poems. The ecstatic, addictive intensity of war's experience is well-known-enough, though our admissions about its pleasures have typically been censured and repressed. Soldiers have always, even now, found battle and war intoxicating, profound, and haunting. Its intensity seems to tap into the same deep levels of the psyche as sexual experience, and the confusion of the two realms (darkly evident, of course, in military rape) has often been represented in literature. In the temporary madness of Achilles depicted in the *Iliad*, the hero slaughters a herd of cattle, believing them to be enemy soldiers. On another level, the fraternity of military life answers a deep thirst for masculine identity which is as present in the souls of modern men as it was in earlier ages.

In Apollinaire's case, the poet's great natural resources of temperament infused all his experience, even his failures, with a romantic appreciation ("a dying love is the sweetest," he wrote). If there is something childlike in these transformations of battle into lyric poetry, Apollinaire's appreciation for the war also represents a calculated, lifelong dedication to wonder, asserting its equality to anything. "Be afraid," he says in his poem "Victory," "that someday a train will no longer thrill you / Look at it faster for your own sake." In the poem "Guerre" (War), his gusto for technology is spookily prescient; in the poet's allegorical imagination, the fantastic paraphernalia of modern warfare seems to promise a kind of impending spiritual freedom. In Apollinaire's psychic process, no division exists between machine and vision; to him, the noise of gunfire is also the sound of the approaching future:

> Central combat sector
>   Contact by sound
> We're firing towards "noises that were heard"
> The young men of the class of 1915
> And those electrified wires
> Then don't weep for the horrors of war
> Before the war we had only the surface
> Of the earth and the seas
> After it we'll have the depths
> Subterranean and aerial space
> Masters of the helm
> After after
> We'll assume all the joys
> Of conquerors in repose

("Guerre")

The most uncanny aspect of Apollinaire's war poems, collected in *Calligrammes*, is their erotic energy. For Apollinaire, as for his immediate successors, the Surrealists (though that label had not yet been coined) all experience was infiltrated with romantic sexuality. The surrealist ethos dictated that Eros provided access to mystery and the unconscious. Romantic longing for the hypothetical other was the catalytic agent of the creative spirit. Marcel Duchamp, his avant-garde contemporary, used the name "Rrose Sélavy" as one of his artistic pseudonyms, a homonym for "Eros c'est la vie." It is not surprising that, even during his two years of military exile, Apollinaire managed to be engaged to several women, sometimes mailing the same love poem to more than one address. The declaration of love was the password into the kingdom of poetry. And so Apollinaire sees, in the bursting of flares, an affair that might end in death—but, nonetheless, an affair. The bombs remove their brassieres, and make available both love and death:

Two flares
Rose explosion
Like two breasts unbound
Raising their nipples insolently
HE KNEW HOW TO LOVE
    what an epitaph

("Festival")

But the Eros in Apollinaire's war poems—so French, so avant-garde, so romantic—was disquieting even to some of his most ardent friends. His descriptions of battle, which mingled lust and wonder, seemed, to Louis Aragon, who wrote an editorial on the subject, indecent. "It would be a crime to show the attractive face of war," wrote Aragon in a public reproach, "even if it had one."

That link, between Eros and war, is easy to censure; for good reason it makes us uneasy. Confronted with the beginning of Apollinaire's great poem, "Wonder of War," what would widows and humanists make of the poet's description of bombardment? In these images of bombardment, they might at first find something to recognize, but then, in its mordant oracular rapture, they would be moved towards more troubled recognitions:

How lovely these flares are that light up the dark
They climb their own peak and lean down to look
They are dancing ladies whose glances become eyes arms
    and hearts

. . . .

It's also the daily apotheosis of all my Berenices whose hair
    has turned to comets' tails
These dancing girls twice gilded belong to all times and all
    races
Swiftly they give birth to children who have just time enough
    to die

The canonical benchmark for twentieth-century war poetry
has often been ascribed to the work of Wilfred Owen, poems
written on a different front of the same war. (The two poets died
within five days of each other in 1918.) Owen's poetry embodies the shock and moral repugnance that has been the better
known model for how poetry should respond to civilized violence. And Owen's romantic story, as well-known as his poems,
has come down to us as a parable about the transforming effect
of history on innocence: how the young British soldier went to
war as a maker of flowery verse and came back a poet of moral
rage and insight. Owen's poetics of horror and pity seem to testify to how reality disciplines language itself.

But there are different kinds of knowing to be gathered from
the war poems of Apollinaire, who went to war as a chanteur of
love and celebration, and, apparently unchastened by experience, grew more rapturous and ecstatic than ever. In "Wonder
of War," one of Apollinaire's greatest poems, the poet seems to
be not down on the field, but high in the bleachers, cheering on
this huge spectacle of wasteful violence, in which he sees the ritual engagement of grand, primeval forces: the devouring earth-
mother who gives and takes back everything in orgiastic ecstasy.

I seem to be at a great feast lighted *a giorno*
A banquet that the earth offers herself
Hungrily she opens her long pale mouths
Earth is hungry and here is the feast

It is his mythological, visionary consciousness which transforms one reality into another, and celebrates the surging archetypal energies released even in this display of destructiveness. This mythological consciousness does not distinguish in absolute terms between Eros and Thanatos; both are the processes of the monumental, omnivorous life of Earth.

> How lovely all these flares are
> But it would be finer if there were still more of them
> If there were millions with a full and relative meaning like
> letters in a book
> However it's as lovely as if life itself issued from those who
> are dying
>
> But it would be finer still if there were still more of them

This is not the French poet, but the ravenous earth-mother speaking, both horrible and wonderful. In his ecstatic transport, the poet relishes the climax of battle. Yet there is also a mournful, visionary compassion in Apollinaire's poem, an acknowledgement of the grotesque inhumanity of the spectacle. In a subsequent, even more Whitmanesque passage, the poet exceeds his own physical boundaries, and heroically flows into the myriad physical elements of the battlefield, an imaginative act which is both chillingly unnatural and heroically tender:

> But I have flowed into the sweetness of this war with my
> whole company along the long trenches
> A few cries of flame keep announcing my presence
> I have hollowed out the bed where I flow and branch into a
> thousand small streams going everywhere
> I am in the front-line trenches and still I am everywhere or
> rather I am beginning to be everywhere
> For it is I who begin this affair of the centuries to come
> It will be longer to realize than the myth of soaring Icarus
>
> I bequeath to the future the story of Guillaume Apollinaire
> Who was in the war and knew how to be everywhere
> In the lucky towns behind the front lines
> In all the rest of the universe

In those who died tangled in the barbed wire
In women in cannons in horses

In this cosmic climax, destruction and reunion are strangely, poignantly conjoined. Apollinaire's identification of his own prophetic powers, so completely realized here, runs throughout his work; such passages can be startling because they exist in such fluent continuity with his other, more mortal registers— the charming, socially amicable voice, for example. But Apollinaire is a true shape-changer, or *leaper*, who springs from role to role, from level to level of poetic possibility. Perhaps the intensely religious sensibility evident in Apollinaire's descriptions, which can be traced back to his Catholic upbringing by nuns, created a capacity for visionary meaning even in death. Liberated by modernity from confinement to one doctrine, his spirituality finds itself heroically adaptable and confident. In his poem "On Prophecies," he explains to his friend:

Everybody is a prophet my dear André Billy
But for so long people have been made to believe
They have no future and are ignorant forever
            And born idiots
That they've become resigned . . .
There's nothing religious in any of these matters
In the superstitions or in the prophecies
Or in anything that people call the occult
There is above all a way of observing nature . . .
Which is completely legitimate

In March 1916, while reading a newspaper in the trench, Apollinaire was struck by a flying piece of shrapnel, which pierced his helmet. He realized he had been wounded only when blood dripped onto his paper. The shrapnel was extracted, but his condition complicated; he was trepanned at a battlefield hospital, and eventually sent back to Paris. Released from the military, he resumed his literary life in Paris, at last a fully illustrious figure among the painters and writers of his time. In the next year he saw projects to completion, coined the seminal term *surrealism* and wrote his manifesto "The New Spirit," as well as "The Pretty

Redhead." But accounts suggest that he was a diminished version of his former self, and in November of 1918, one week before the armistice, which ended the war, Apollinaire succumbed to another attack, the influenza epidemic that was sweeping, at that moment, the entire Western world.

Apollinaire's poetry still enjoys great popularity. His love of urban particularity, his pastiche of common and lofty tones, his spontaneous intelligence and his rowdy effervescence all make him peculiarly appealing to American readers. Lovers of the convivial, sprinting poems of Frank O'Hara are unwittingly sampling the texture of Apollinaire. His most anthologized poems—"Zone" and "The Pretty Redhead"—are deservedly canonical, the first for its dramatic exhibition of modernist technique, the second for its profound, droll, and lucid exposition of aesthetics.

Yet Apollinaire's war poems are less well-known than one would expect. They challenge the reader who would segregate ethical understanding and imaginative wildness. These poems, however, are insistently astonishing—never jaded, and paradoxically wholesome. They tell a story about the unquenchable capacity of the human imagination, which roams outside prescribed boundaries, and finds delight and humor even in the middle of suffering. In his poem "Il y a" (There Is There Are) he exercises one of his favorite poetic devices, simultaneism. The strategy of simultaneism is to catalogue the manifold possible contents of a single moment—a modernism of wonder. In poems like this, Apollinaire shows the vigorous, anguished expansiveness that keeps him relevant. The poem is part celebration, part lament, and it models the inclusive compassionate sensibility which makes this poet part of the heroic tradition in modernism; an explorer of the future who still seems utterly contemporary:

> There are Barbary figs on the cactus in Algeria
> There are my love's long supple hands
> There's an inkwell I made in a 15-centimeter rocket they
>   didn't send off
> There's my saddle out in the rain
> There are the rivers that won't flow uphill again . . .

There are men in the world who have never been to war
There are Hindus watching in astonishment the Western
    landscapes
They think sadly of their friends and wonder if they'll see
    them again
For we have pushed very far in this war the art of invisibility

The Pursuit of Ignorance
The Challenging Figuration of Not Knowing

The end-virtue of humility comes only after a long train
of humiliations; and the chief labor of humbling is the
constant, resourceful restoration of ignorance.
— R. P. Blackmur

The greatest human intellectual achievement of the twentieth
century was the discovery of how fucking clueless we human beings are. Or, no, not *clueless*, exactly, but let us say "vision-limited"
or "insight-impaired" or "in the dark." All our quantum mechan-
ics, our frozen pizzas, our electric cars and nation states are just
whistling in the dark. Most of our earthly success as a species is
just evidence that we've been promoted above the actual level of
our competence.

In the twentieth century we also came to understand that our
relentless acquisition of "knowledge" and "information" does
very little to decrease the degree of our ignorance. Paradoxically, education often serves only to increase our delusions of
mastery—and that very confidence decreases our sensitivity to
the presence of the unknowable.

Although this realization that we are in the dark creates an
ache in the modern heart, it is also one of the most positive
and powerful of insights. Potentially, it can inspire humility, caution, wonder, and respect for our profoundly limited grasp of
the real. Every vision, we now know, has a periphery and beyond
that there is, well, nobody knows: much, much more dark.

This revelation of our unknowingness also created (and creates) a great challenge for contemporary artists. Consider how

difficult it is to make a concise image for *not-knowing*! How difficult it is to craft a statement that does not merely conceptualize, or smugly insinuate that the speaker has mastered the fact of her own non-understanding? Some of the greatest modernist writers – Beckett and Eliot and Woolf—dedicated themselves to representing that remarkable aspect of the human condition: an artistic job that, on the one hand, must be executed with the subtlety of a hint; on the other, delivered with enough rude force to crack our default setting of sleep.

Happily, in fact, there have been many poetic successes in this slippery task of making real our existential confusion. The best of them constitute, for me, a special and fascinating genre, and they could be assembled into an anthology: "Images of Ignorance."

Dante's opening lines to *The Inferno* are the most canonical of such testimonies. If our *Anthology of Ignorance* existed, his lines would open it: "Midway in life's journey," says Dante, "I woke to find myself in a dark wood." In my anthology, however, our own Ralph Waldo Emerson would exceed him. In his essay "Experience," Emerson, that rare man whose character united brilliance and a remarkable lack of egotism, pretty much nails it:

> We wake and find ourselves on a stair; there are stairs below us which we seem to have ascended, and there are stairs above us, many a one, which go upwards and out of sight . . . Sleep lingers all our lifetime about our eyes, as night hovers all day in the boughs of the fir tree. All things swim and glitter.

Emerson's image is a perfect distillation of what they used to call *the human condition*—and it does what good metaphors do, providing us with a concise visual correlative for what would otherwise be impossible to comprehend: our uncanny position in the middle of a life we don't really understand. We are haunted and baffled by where we are in time, our lack of memory, and notionless as to where we are going; but Emerson's image, and the sentence in which it is embedded, situates us lucidly without simplifying things in the slightest. It is so good it can make a reader genuinely dizzy.

An early poem by W. S. Merwin, "The Gods," undertakes the

challenge of representing human ignorance through a kind of parable:

> My blind neighbor has required of me
> A description of darkness
> And I begin I begin . . .

Tasked with the oddest of commissions, the speaker only gradually realizes that darkness is not describable to someone who lives solely inside it. In this way, the speaker realizes that he himself is blind and unable to describe his own condition. Linguistically, he discovers he does not possess a vocabulary with which to pick this thing up. The fumbling repetition, "I begin I begin," with its eloquent inarticulateness, insinuates that he can barely begin this work—and could never finish. Such performances of language breakdown—and of the failure of words—have been one of the most reliable modernist tropes devised to signify the limit of human knowing. The inability to speak well serves as an emblem of standing on a precipice. This—to come to the edge of the precipice, and stop, and look out from it, to bring the reader to the existential cusp, where speech fails—is a highly refined artistic act.

Here's how the Beat poet Lew Welch captured it, in a more sweetly instructional and plainspoken manner than Merwin or Emerson:

> Step out onto the planet.
> Draw a circle a hundred feet round.
> Inside the circle are
> 300 things nobody understands, and, maybe nobody's ever
>   really seen.
> How many can you find?

Tomas Tranströmer might be the greatest twentieth-century poet of ignorance. The entire body of Tranströmer's work seems deeply, intently focused on exploring and articulating correlatives for being half-awake in the midst of mystery. Again and again, his poems remind us of the shadowed side of consciousness and life, the bottomless chasm under our own feet. One can visit any page in his work and find pungent and complex images for the presence of the invisible, and for the struggle within us between refusal and acceptance of our ignorance. A few lines from Tranströmer's poem "Nocturne" (translated by Robert Bly) may illustrate:

> I lie about to fall asleep, I see unknown images
> and signs sketching themselves behind the eyelids
> on the wall of the dark. In the slot between waking and sleep
> a large letter tries to get in without quite succeeding.

That letter, trying to squeeze through the mail delivery slot— What is it? What message does it contain? In Tranströmer's animistic and Jungian-inflected version of the world, there are strange forces at loose, both natural and supernatural—fog, trees, and houses—that reach out and prod us, trying to wake us to the collective, immersive mystery.

Tranströmer himself was a professional psychologist, and his descriptions of human ignorance shift their emphasis from the vocabulary of existential estrangement toward a more psychic and occult construct, in which consciousness is itself a vast city, a compartmentalized metropolis we dwell in but know little about. It may be ours, but we are more strangers here than we think.

In "Streets in Shanghai," (translated by Samuel Charters) Tranströmer describes the densely packed streets of that city, and the way the populace is as full of unconscious energies as the streets are of people:

> At dawn the running crowds set our silent planet going.
> Then the park fills with people. For each one eight faces
>   polished like jade, for all situations, to avoid mistakes.
> For each one also the invisible face that reflects "something
>   you don't talk about."
> Something that emerges in tired moments and is as pungent
>   as a sip of Viper schnapps, with its long, scaly aftertaste.

One reason for the complex resonance of Tranströmer's images is that they are drawn from different psychological models of selfhood. Anxious, self-protective, compartmentalized, dissembling—each human being has at least eight different faces, some of which are concealed and some of which are brought out to confront and deceive the world. The Freudian model is here, all right. But in a Tranströmer poem additional mystical forces are at work as well. The enigmatic concluding section of "Streets in Shanghai" makes human beings look like players in a kind of cosmic theater:

> Behind each one walking here hovers a cross that wants to
> catch up to us, pass us, join us.
> Something that wants to sneak up on us from behind and
> cover our eyes and whisper, "Guess who?"

> We look almost happy out in the sun, while we bleed to
> death from wounds we know nothing about.

What art Tranströmer displays at moments like this! His images for the unconscious character of our lives are both precise and mysterious, both spooky and playful; he knows that our collectively opaque condition is in some sense incurable; yet the poem's closing declaration is a cry of compassion, wonder, distress, and understanding. One senses old ideologies wandering around in the existential dark, the lingering haunts of Christian and perhaps pagan realities. In Tranströmer's world, human beings are often depicted as shallow, and possessed of only diminished vision, but the world we walk through is also inhabited by various kinds of intangible, powerful sentience: "Guess who?"

An essay on this topic could be long and analytical and learned. But when it comes to the topic of ignorance, it seems wise to be brief, and simply to say that we are always on the verge of falling asleep, always in need of a pinch to wake us to our actual condition.

It is the poet's charge to keep guessing about the nature of that condition, and about our own darkness and outlying territories. Recognizing our ignorance, we find richer hues of incomprehension—a feeling not to be conquered, but explored, and possibly extended. Perhaps the bravest and most useful poet of any time is the one who can locate and record her own urgent inner voice, that voice whispering *Stop. Wake up. Guess Who?*

The Power of Coldness

Rain that pours down in the tropics, in the late afternoon, from those bruise-colored, low-hanging galleons of cloud, is wet and warm, but when rain falls from high in the upper stratosphere, even on a hot day, it is wonderfully, almost exotically chilled when it strikes your face and arms. You feel that it has travelled to you from a distant realm, a place far away and very different from ours. And some poetry is like that as well—brisk and bracing.

Coldness, one of the more intriguing powers of poetry, is a specialized skill, and an essential element in the work of certain poets. "Cast a cold eye on life, on death," advises Yeats, but in the craft of poetry few skills are harder to master. Poetic coldness requires a gift for iconoclastic objectivity, plus a talent for acerbic formulation. "I have seen this swan and / I have seen you;" says Marianne Moore. "I have seen ambition without / understanding in a variety of forms." Brrrr.

Compressed and analytical, forceful yet detached, coldness broadcasts along a particular wavelength of sensibility. Coldness penetrates, yet it is not willfully shocking or aggressive. Coldness does not hope, demand, or expect that human nature can be altered.

Many of the greatest poems ("Dover Beach," "Ode on Melancholy") undertake to defend the realm of emotion from the soulless pragmatics of the rational, and this is, of course, a crucial mission. But coldness observes, deduces, and names what it sees. It attempts to enunciate and, in addition, dissect the facts, even if they are unsympathetic. In the art of coldness, accuracy has precedence over tact.

The inclination for coldness is not terrifically common. Most poets steer clear of this territory, perhaps because they recognize that certain observations can come off as uncharitable, didactic, or perhaps even deliberately offensive in a show-offy, adolescent way. It is an open secret that in our therapeutic era, many poets are attempting not just to write a poem, but to be loved for it as well. More poets serve comfort food than icicles. To be genuinely chilly is to place audience approval in jeopardy, and to forgo the seductive manners of intimacy that contemporary poems are often invested in. The cold speaker does not ask for the reader's agreement or permission; in this way, perhaps, true poetic coldness might be said to be the slightest bit misanthropic.

Szymborska's Forensics: An Argument against Empathy

In Wisława Szymborska's "The Suicide's Room," the speaker itemizes the contents of a recently vacated apartment and seems to be seeking the reason for this dead person's choice to kill himself. Immediately, she targets our assumptions about the suicide victim's circumstances:

> I'll bet you think the room was empty.
> Wrong. There were three chairs with sturdy backs.
> A lamp, good for fighting off the dark.

The striking dimension of Szymborska's poem is the relentless detachment of its interrogation. In its analytical inventory, it offers little of the conventional sympathy or pathos we might expect from the situation. Instead, Szymborska's poem is forensic, which means systematic and analytical. Methodical in its investigation, it is more dedicated to the facts than the feelings. Considering the man's desperation, she writes, "No way out? But what about the door? / No prospects? The window had other views."

In much of Szymborska's poetry, the emotion of wonder seems to be her strategic response to the paradoxical nature of experience. By contrast, "The Suicide's Room" is a worldly, grounded thing. Ultimately, the speaker wishes to force us to look harder and more closely, more skeptically at the facts, and the evidence suggests that the suicide was prosperous in the things of the world. He had:

A desk, and on the desk a wallet, some newspapers.
A carefree Buddha and a worried Christ.
Seven lucky elephants, a notebook in a drawer. . . .

Joy the spark of gods.
Odysseus stretched on the shelf in life-giving sleep
after the labors of Book Five.

It's interesting to observe how conventional and automatic
our own default instincts for psychological reading are. Just as
Szymborska's speaker studies the evidence of the suicide's outer
life for clues about the inner life, we naturally, habitually scan
the surface of the poem for evidence of the speaker's "true" feelings. Sure, we say, the speaker sounds cold, but how, we ask, does
she really feel about this loss? We try to read through the surface of the poem for traces of the speaker's "actual" feelings—
bitterness? grief? Yet maybe, in this case, that wounded under-
surface isn't there. Perhaps this disappearance is not even a
tragedy, because "tragedy" would imply that some great connection once existed between the departed and his survivors. In this
case, says the speaker, we might as well save our tears.

It might even be said that the poem is engaged in an unusual
enterprise, one specifically related to poetic coldness. It is foren-
sically dismantling the mechanism of empathy itself. Not so fast
with your grief, the poet's tone suggests, with your imaginative
projection, and melodrama. Empathy might not be called for
here; don't rush past the details to the presumption of feelings,
which often serve as an abdication of intellect. In this case, the
human being remains a mystery, but perhaps not an especially
interesting or revealing one. Szymborska concludes,

His glasses
lay on the windowsill.
And one fly buzzed—that is, was still alive.

You think at least the note must tell us something.
But what if I say there was no note—
and he had so many friends, but all of us fit neatly
inside the empty envelope propped up against a cup.

In that closing pronoun, "us," we may detect some grievance on the part of the speaker—"all of us fit neatly inside the empty envelope"—but if so, it is a faint, austere whisper. To encounter such stark description in a poem is an opportunity to confront not our human nature but existence itself. Szymborska's poem ends, one might say, not with a bang or a whimper, but a kind of shrug. That's the cold eye at work.

Miłosz's Cold Iconoclasm

Czesław Miłosz's poem "Merchants" also seems anthropological in its objective, penetrating account of human behavior. "Merchants" surveys humankind, that peculiar species, with great detachment, and Miłosz's particular topic—the quaint religious practices of Homo sapiens—is intriguing. The poem begins:

> In a town where a miracle occurred, merchants install their
>   booths,
> side by side, along a street through which pilgrims proceed.
>
> They display their goods, wondering at the stupidity which
>   compels
> people to buy little crosses, tiny medals, rosaries.
>
> Even plastic bottles in the shape of the Madonna for
>   preservation of
> the healing waters.

The poem, we initially suspect, is going to be an editorial on greed: the exploitation of the pious by the avaricious, the profit motive contrasted to the yearning for the divine, the wealthy versus the disenfranchised. Yet Miłosz's speaker maintains an omniscient, reportorial distance from the scene, and a matter-of-fact tone. The depiction of the vendors is severe, but it's detached rather than judgmental.

Our expectation is equally subverted by the narrator's clinical description of the downtrodden believers. These may be pilgrims, the speaker says, but they fail to impress. They seem less like courageous soldiers of faith than constitutionally chronic weaklings, and what is notable is the poem's cool, leveling indifference toward all its characters. Miłosz's speaker trains his keen, appraising intellect equally upon the devout and the calculating avaricious:

> the sick on their stretchers, the paralyzed in their
> wheelchairs
>
> Fortify the merchants in their disdainful belief that religion
> is self-consolation, based on the understandable need for
> any kind of rescue.
>
> They rub their hands, reckon, add to their inventory new
> supplies of crucifixes, or nickel coins imprinted with the
> effigies of popes.
>
> And the pilgrims, looking at their faces, onto which have
> crept scarcely noticeable smiles, feel threatened in their
> faith, just as children feel threatened by grown-ups,
> keepers of a secret, guessed at, but still vague.

The scene recalls, of course, the biblical narrative, the vulnerable "Christians" versus the cold-blooded, profiteering "Romans." The salesmen wonder "at the stupidity which compels people to buy little crosses." Yet the speaker's assessing eye does not stop with the implicit judgment of the easily vilified merchants. They may be smug in their conviction that religion is "self-consolation." But the poem's last two couplets especially surprise us, with their ruthless assessment of the needy Christians. In this diminished world, the faithful, clearly fallen from grace, are depicted as merely—pitifully—childlike; whereas the more worldly but jaded salesmen represent a tarnished version of what it might mean to be adult. Neither sample of humanity is admirable, and the reader is not encouraged to identify with either group. We are left to hang precariously on the outside of this tableau. Though Miłosz may not give us what we have come to expect from poetry—a comfortable humanist superiority, or a consoling, clear-cut version of good and bad—his survey of human motives is meticulous, penetrating, and damning, a window into the perennially flawed nature of humanity.

Henri Cole's Coldness of Understatement

Henri Cole's poem "Oil & Steel" displays the strategic advantage of treating an autobiographical subject with great coldness. The death of the speaker's father is the poem's occasion, one that seems justifiably, almost unavoidably charged with feeling, but Cole's poem achieves its power not by emoting, but by reporting the grim intimate details with a hard-boiled, matter-of-fact objectivity.

This cool lucidity, rather than holding the reader outside of the poem, paradoxically draws us close to the narrative. Left unsaid, the speaker's feelings—expressed as neither grievance, anger, nor sorrow—exude more force than would a conventional treatment. It does no harm that Cole has an aptitude for vivid, unglamorous facts. Here is the whole of Cole's poem:

> My father lived in a dirty-dish mausoleum,
> watching a portable black-and-white television,
> reading the Encyclopedia Britannica,
> which he preferred to Modern Fiction.
> One by one, his schnauzers died of liver disease,
> except the one that guarded his corpse
> found holding a tumbler of Bushmills.
> "Dead is dead," he would say, an anti-preacher.
> I took a plaid shirt from the bedroom closet
> and some motor oil—my inheritance.
> Once, I saw him weep in a courtroom—
> neglected, needing nursing—this man who never showed
> me much affection but gave me a knack
> for solitude, which has been mostly useful.

Terseness, it turns out, is one technique for rendering poetic coldness, and Cole's speaker uses it by withholding affect from the story he tells. When he says, "I took a plaid shirt from the bedroom closet / and some motor oil—my inheritance," the delivery is so deadpan that it is both comedic and bitter. We say that some remarks are spoken "dryly"—this reportage is both emotionally dehydrated and freeze-dried.

The syntax of sentence two is worth study in itself for the way it embodies emotional distance. Grammatically, the main noun-verb is the death of the dogs—"his schnauzers died." But in contrast, the father's death is relegated to a subordinate clause. Grammar here enacts a cold, in its way, contemptuous psychological displacement. On a psychological level we also can see that the speaker's coldness is an unconscious emulation of the father-figure, a man who would say, "Dead is dead." The closing lines of "Oil & Steel" are a sort of summit of chilliness, in which the speaker reports, "Once I saw him weep in a courtroom— / neglected, needing nursing—this man . . ." The shift in diction from "father" to "this man" similarly indicates the stoical detachment of the speaker from his father.

Cole's poem could be studied as a textbook on the deployment of a cold temperament, and as an advertisement for the power of a cold poetics. For, in its way, it displays the intellectual, and even the human, triumphs of detachment. The poem concludes with a declaration of gratitude for the compensating consequences of deprivation. Here is a speaker with such self-possession that he can express thanks for his inheritance, that "knack for solitude," and a lack of expectation of more. Such clarity is a useful adaptation, though its limitations are hinted at in the word "mostly." Self-pity, if it is here at all, is barely audible.

Ultimately, our mastery of different tones in life amounts to the acquisition of utilitarian skills. In that sense, coldness in poetry is a valuable and a truly interesting poetic property. One could hypothesize that it is a skill that appears late in the evolution of the self and even late in the history of a given culture. Poetic coldness is an inheritance that arrives long after the Wordsworthian, joyful Romantic child has been plunged into the world, betrayed and outlived. The analytic clarity is a more adult dimension of character, a self-possession, and as it appears in poems like these, it amounts to a genuine and durable gift to the rest of us. Coldness shows us how to stand back, watch, listen, think. Coldness is like the presence of elders.

"I Live My Life in Growing Orbits"
Robert Bly as Role Model

Now the Chief Executive enters; the press conference
    begins:
First the President lies about the date the Appalachian
    Mountains rose.
Then he lies about the population of Chicago, then he
    lies about the weight of the adult eagle, then about the
    acreage of the Everglades

He lies about the number of fish taken every year in the
    Arctic, he has private information about which city *is* the
    capital of Wyoming, he lies about the birthplace of Attila
    the Hun.

He lies about the composition of the amniotic fluid, and he
    insists that Luther was never a German, and that only the
    Protestants sold indulgences,

. . . .

And the Attorney General lies about the time the sun sets.
       —Robert Bly, "The Teeth Mother Naked at Last"

When I first read this passage from Robert Bly's collection, *Sleepers Joining Hands* some thirty-five years ago, I think I learned something about wild hilarity, about nerve, and about the power of the imagination to throw off chains. It was a lesson that empowered me, and it is a lesson I hope never to forget as a person and as a poet.

Bly's poem was written against the backdrop of the Vietnam War; it addresses, through its fantastic hyperbole, the political dishonesty of U.S. leadership in that era. The "Chief Executive" of the poem was probably Lyndon Johnson. In its poetics, however, Bly's poem is fascinating for the way it joins together two very different human instincts—our deep desire for justice, and that other appetite, our need for imaginative flight.

That marriage of energies, of imagination and justice, is an unusual combination to find in any poem. It is especially rare in American poetry—for, after all, American culture has never found it easy to reconcile the sobriety of responsibility and the lightness of laughter. As a culture, we believe in keeping our responsibilities and our pleasures separate. They are like different food groups, not to be served on the same plate. It is as if we are afraid they might contaminate each other, that the gravy from the mashed potatoes is going to leak into the string beans. There is some truth in the assertion that American pragmatism has been repressing inspiration for 250 years—simply by saying, "All that laughter and ecstasy, I really don't think it is *practical*, do you?"

Such a segregation of sensibility did not afflict the poet Robert Bly, whose whole life has been a refusal to compartmentalize. Now in his eighties, near the end of a lifetime of prodigious creativity and cultural activism, Bly's life and career present a model worth reviewing. In our era, when American creative writing, especially poetry, has largely sheltered itself inside and around the university system, and in an era in which well-groomed "professionalism" has become a standard for the career writer, Bly's lifework offers an alternative model for what a poet's existence on Planet America might look like.

In the annals of twentieth century poetics, Bly will probably be remembered as the founder of and spokesperson for the mid-century "Deep Image" school of poetry, an aesthetic centered on the power of the associative image. Yet he has been so much more. It would be more accurate to say that Bly was the Ezra Pound of the mid- and late-twentieth century. Like Pound, Bly made enormous contributions as a translator, as a poet, and as a community builder. He was a connector of people, aesthetic movements, and ideas. Gertrude Stein called Pound a "village explainer," and Bly also made himself a conduit between modern American poetry and the larger world. He was an evangelistic popularizer of poetry, a fierce and lifelong political activist, an importer and exporter of ideas and original inspirations, a nomadic pilgrim of aesthetics and poetry possibilities. A list of his seminal books on poetics would include *Leaping Poetry*, *The Little Book of the Human Shadow*, and *American Poetry: Wildness and Domesticity*. His studies of social forces include *Iron John* and *The Sibling Society*.

One particular reason that Bly's life should be of interest to a younger generation is that he has managed to thrive as a poet and writer entirely outside the university system. Although he received a master's degree from the Iowa Writer's workshop in 1956, Bly felt (and frequently declared) that the university was an insular and constraining place, inimical to the poetic imagination; that it did not allow enough wildness of feeling or thought, and diminished the contact with reality that a true poet requires for growth. Though he struggled for many decades to support himself and his family (unlike his contemporary Robert Lowell, Bly did not come from a moneyed background), Bly's life story is one of remarkable autonomy, driven by a curiosity and industry that had little to do with the motivation for conventional success. He lived in a way that persistently mingled the life of art with the world at large. More than any poet of his own generation, except possibly Adrienne Rich, Bly has been a productive and contrarian participant in American culture at large.

Here are a few of many examples of Bly's brashness. In 1967, when Bly was presented with the National Book Award for *The Light Around the Body*, his second collection, he arranged to hand over the prize money to a young American draft resister, and to publicly encourage the young man to burn his draft card—technically a crime against the state. In 1974, Bly taught a course in his hometown called "The Discoveries of Freud and Jung and How They Apply to Life in Madison, Minnesota." In his essay "Where Have All the Critics Gone?" he says, "Harold Bloom teaches poets to wrestle with dead fathers, but it seems to me that it is important for poets to wrestle with, even attack, living fathers and living sons. My own generation of poets . . . has not been attacked enough by younger poets. . . . Being rude to older poets is just a way of clearing ground for yourself."

Bly is one of the generation of American poets born during the 1920s, a group too staggeringly numerous and luminary to list. It was a heroic, ground-breaking generation, which pioneered American free verse, and left a body of work that defined the latter half of the twentieth century. It included writers as various and influential as Frank O'Hara, Adrienne Rich, Galway Kinnell, Sylvia Plath, Philip Levine, Allen Ginsberg, James Merrill, and W. S. Merwin. In the prosperous American years after World War II, these poets came of age with a brash rebellious confidence about the cultural and visionary possibilities of American poetry. Seen from the present moment, such conditions are hard to imagine, but the end result, a remarkable body of important art, is irrefutable and inspiring.

In the 1950s, Bly, along with James Wright and a few others, began a lifelong engagement with translation. Here again, the list is mind-bendingly far-flung and various. He started with Spanish-language poets like Vallejo and Machado, Neruda and Lorca, Juan Ramón Jiménez, Blas de Otero. The German poet Georg Trakl was also among the first to be shepherded into English. In the mid-sixties, Bly translated Swedish poets like Gunnar Ekelöf and Tomas Tranströmer, bringing them to American attention long before their fame (Tranströmer won the Nobel Prize in 2011). "If the Americans do not have European poets to refresh their sense of what association is," said Bly in *Leaping Poetry*, "their work soon falls back into the boring associative tracks that so many followed through the *Kenyon Review Times*, and the dull political landscapes of the *Partisan Review*." It's hard to overestimate how transformative such translation work by Bly and others has been, but it permanently changed the shape and flavor of American poetry. It brought us into an international conversation, which we are still carrying on today.

Viewed from a distance, Bly's work, so diverse and polymorphic, nonetheless has one constant common thread: a passionate assertion of the value of the irrational to Western culture, and of the folly of trying to ignore or repress the unconscious.

To study Bly's own poetic development is to see how he absorbed and was influenced by many of the foreign poets whose work he brought into English. To take one instance, Bly's political critique found an invaluable idiom in the surrealism of the Spanish poets. From the beginning, Bly had been thinking about American history, about power and the nature of culture. Politics are nearly invisible in his pastoral first collection, but by the mid-sixties, he was denouncing what was then called "the military industrial complex" and the role of corporate capitalism in an array of colonial interventions. To look back at some of those poems now, Bly's consciousness of first-world injustice seems notably undated. Here are some stanzas from "Condition of the Working Classes: 1970":

You United States, frightened by dreams of Guatemala,
building houses with eight-mile-long wings to imprison the
    Cubans
eating a bread made of the sound of sunken buffalo bones,
drinking water turned dark by the shadow of Negroes. . . .

Our spirit is inside the baseball rising into the light

So the crippled ships go out onto the deep,
sexual orchids fly out to meet the rain,
    the singer sings from deep in his chest,
memory stops,
        black threads string out in the wind,
the eyes of the nation go blind.

The building across the street suddenly explodes,
wild horses run through the long hair on the ground floor.
Cripple Creek's survivors peer out from an upper-story
    window, blood pours from their ears,
the Sioux dead sleep all night in the rain troughs on the
    Treasury Building.

The poetic antecedents for applying surrealism to political realities existed, in some poems by Lorca and Neruda, but no American poet before Bly had used it quite like this.

Where He Came From: The Auto-Didact from a
Minnesota Farm

If you look at photographs of Robert Bly from the late fifties, you would see a tall gangly fellow with short hair, in a black suit and a skinny tie. He looks like a farmhand dressed for church on Sunday, or like a respectable young insurance adjustor. Raised on a farm in northern Minnesota, in an atmosphere of Protestant severity, he was not bred for sophistication. He grew up in the landscapes of the American prairie, amid the smell of fields and horses, where he was initiated into the knowledge of physical work. After high school, he served two years in the merchant marine, and went to Harvard on the GI Bill. In 1958, when he moved back to Minnesota, he was a poet who had published no books, and had no great reason for self-confidence.

But Bly was already deeply immersed in the work of Carl Jung and the German mystic Jacob Böhme, and he was already a natural born maker of friendship and communities. He was writing letters, and making cold calls to older poets like David Ignatow and Louis Simpson. As Ignatow recalls it, one day the phone rang at his office; he picked it up, and someone on the other end said, "My name is Robert Bly and I think that you're an important American poet. I want to come and talk to you about your work." Robert Bly was a nobody, but he was a nobody who soon was starting a magazine called *The Fifties*, a nobody who had commenced his lifelong practice of issuing pronouncements on the state of American poetry. He was already denouncing the reign of T. S. Eliot and the scholasticism of the New Critics. He was reading international poetry, and advocating a more exultant and daring vision of American poetry, and a connection to the world at large that we take for granted today. The first issue of his magazine, *The Fifties*, published in 1958, contained poems by Gary Snyder, Louis Simpson, Gunnar Ekelöf, and Henri Michaux; translations from Swedish, Danish, and French. It featured an editorial by an irascible imaginary critic named Crunk, and a blurb on the back cover that said: "Strontium 90 builds strong bones for Halloween."

If one preeminent lesson can be gleaned from Bly's career, it would be this: he did not *compartmentalize* the different parts

101

of himself, as do most of us. He did not segregate the various imperatives in his life, did not keep the aesthetic apart from the political, the political apart from the spiritual, or the spiritual apart from the aesthetic. Rather, he combined them, and all his life he kept them in ardent interplay. In his book *The Sibling Society*, Bly says that great literature asks us to keep our defiance *and* our laughter; that great literature enables us to exult in the midst of flatness. "Our vigor," he says, "cannot be sustained by giving into the victim-emotions—self-pity, passivity, blaming, or claims for exemption."

This restlessness, this constant changing of coordinates, this self-reinvention, guided by internal necessity and curiosity—that surely must be the best kind of courage one can have. Bly was never "objectively detached" or "disinterested." Nor was he ever still. By the time he reached the 1970s, Bly no longer looked like an insurance adjustor. He had let his hair grow long and shaggy; he was no longer wearing a nice grey suit and tie, but a serape, and at his sensational public readings he would wear frightening shamanic masks as he performed poems that embodied the psychic energies of the Indian deity Kali, and the aboriginal archetype known as the Tooth Mother. Bly's poetic imagery had entered into a period of shamanic surrealism. His performances were wild, passionate with ideas, and often lasted three hours. The countercultural sixties and the seventies were the first era of large public poetry readings, and Bly's readings were packed.

Outsider Status

What did staying outside of academia do for Robert Bly? It allowed him, as William Blake advises, to create his own system, rather than be enslaved by another's. When English departments everywhere were striving to employ the terminology of Eliot and the New Critics, arguing about the seven types of ambiguity and the meaning of the "objective correlative," Bly was speaking of "soul," and "psyche" of the "prehensile image," and *archetype* and *animus*. While literary theorists found increasingly abstruse ways to describe literature, Bly was learning to think in the vocabulary of mystics and psychologists. He described poets in terms of temperature and color, what "brain" they spoke from, and what body of the imagination they inhabited.

Bly's attention evolved and changed directions many times over. Over the next three decades, he deepened his inquiry into European myth, folklore, and storytelling, and the kinds of psychic knowledge they contained. He began associating with Jungians like James Hillman, Marion Woodman, and Joseph Campbell; and storytellers like Gioa Timpanelli. He studied mythopoetics and Jung, and the cultural belief systems of premodern cultures. In 1975, he founded The Great Mother Conference, an annual seminar and culture festival of women and men to discuss mythopoetics in the context of American and international society. The GMC conference is still vibrant and functional today.

Bly's translation work provided him not just with income-producing labor, but with a sequence of mentors and influences which facilitated his own evolution, both aesthetic and psychic. The creative profit of that effort is reflected in Bly's own poems. Reading Bly's work makes clear how particular periods of productivity are the result of his deep immersion in the work of Rilke or Tranströmer, Lorca or Kabir. If the life of close reading is a tutorial, as it is, you could say that Bly studied surreal imagery with Lorca and visualization from Tranströmer; later he learned the art of the parable from Kabir, and the techniques of paradox and dialectic from Hafez.

In the last several decades of his writing life, his study of Sufi ecstatic poetry especially transformed his own work; he devised for himself an "American ghazal" form which managed to combine the unconscious freedom of wild imagery, and the discriminating higher intellect of a person cooked by a lifetime of experience. In this mode, he eventually wrote many of the best poems of his life.

The Poet as Culture Warrior

When one is engaged in a serious investigation of why modern culture is so screwed up, the topic of gender is an inevitable encounter. In the 1980s, Bly began to focus his thinking on the

state of the masculine psyche in Western culture, the male legacy of stoicism, and the worship of power that makes war possible.
Drawing on his own personal history and emotional experience,
he began to explore the emotional numbness which leaves no
direction for the soul but competition, envy, and ambition.

The eventual result of these studies was a book on men's psychology, *Iron John*, and it carried the poet into a realm of unexpected controversy and celebrity. *Iron John* rose to notoriety
on the *New York Times* bestseller list. It was widely discussed and
satirized by many of the media's talking heads, and it was de-
nounced by many well-known feminists, as if the development
of men was in some way in competition with the development
of women. Many jokes were made about men drumming in
the woods, and getting in touch with their inner caveman. In
a climate of expanding feminist consciousness, many people
seemed to feel that the men of the world needed no further
encouragement; they were already over-developed. Yet the book
became a bestseller, and an influential cultural document in
the conversation about gender—and it initiated a long-overdue
conversation about the internal toxicity of masculinity. Read today, *Iron John* still seems far-sighted, compassionate, smart, and
important. Bly's clear, discriminating prose style also makes this
book intensely readable. The same is true of his second book of
cultural analysis, *The Sibling Society*.

When Bly began to publicly consider matters of American
culture at large, something happened that should be of interest
to all of us given to the vocation of poetry as it is practiced in
America. He had become a public intellectual as well as a poet;
in fact, he became popular, and for all of these things he paid
a price.

Among the literary establishment and the tribe of other American poets, Bly was treated with skepticism and resentment. In
the view of the professional elite, poetry is about the cultivation
of aesthetics and technique. What qualifications did Robert Bly,
they asked, possess to have opinions and make judgments about
history and the nature of families? What kind of presumption
was this? It might be acceptable to write a nice essay about the
metrics of free verse, or the esoteric considerations of the frag-
ment, but don't write about the fragmentation of the American

family, don't write about the white fear of men with dark skin. Bly's reward for venturing into the conversation of the culture at large was a kind of literary exile. He was never really allowed back in—but he was playing a larger game, that of a public intellectual, of a culture-gatherer and transmitter.

I can remember the condescension and patronizing tone of my own college writing professor towards this theatrical grandstander, this show-off, Robert Bly. My teacher's underlying assumption, which he communicated to his students, was that someone so various, so flamboyant, and publicly activist must not be a serious poet. Perhaps the implication, or the unconscious subtext, was that Bly was making the rest of us, by comparison, look less alive.

That ascetic, patronizing discomfort with the idea of a larger mission for poetry is still strong among many poets. "There is a terrible, mean American resentment," wrote Susan Sontag, "toward a writer who tries to do many things."

Ambassador of Poetry

Whether he talked about war, or the dysfunctional male, or the mythic passage through the underworld, Bly brought poetry with him as a vehicle for his thinking and his talking. Wherever he went, and whatever he wrote, it was poetry that furnished the illustrations, the images and enactments for that thought. Thus his audiences, whether they wanted to or not, went away with a fresh comprehension that poetry was a distinctive functional language for seeing, understanding, and thinking; they went away opened to the actuality of the living word. It is not enough to say that Bly was a "popularizer" of poetry, but that he was a theologian, a John the Baptist, an embodiment of its powers. Bly practiced what he preached. This passage about Tranströmer illustrates Bly's metaphorical discursive style:

> One of the most beautiful qualities in his poems is the space we feel in them. I think one reason for that is that the four or five main images that appear in his poems come from widely separated sources in the psyche. His poems are a sort of

railway station where trains that have come from enormous distances stand briefly in the same building. One train may have some Russian snow still lying on the undercarriage, and another may have some Mediterranean flowers still fresh in the compartments, and Ruhr soot on the roofs. The poems are mysterious because of the distance the images have come to get there.

To read Bly's prose is to meet a person who is using poetry and literature as a kind of physician, or physic, to treat his own illnesses; to minister to one condition or shortcoming of the soul after another. A persistent focus that runs through all of Bly's thinking is the notion of psychic development: not just that of the individual, but of whole cultures and eras. Bly always saw history itself as a kind of endless struggle between forces in the human soul. Human ideologies and actions are often driven by unconscious fears and unexamined influences. The masculine fear of feeling, for example, is the basis for war and imperialism. Sexism, at bottom, is an expression of the archaic terror of attachment. And Bly very much saw poetry as a powerful means of unearthing and igniting the deep sources of the self:

> It's all right if this suffering goes on for years.
> It's all right if the hawk never finds his own nest.
> It's all right if we never receive the love we want. . . .
>
> It's all right if we can't remain cheerful all day.
> The task we have accepted is to go down
> To renew our friendship with the ruined things.
>
> It's all right if people think we are idiots.
> It's all right if we lie face down on the earth.
> It's all right if we open the coffin and climb in.
>
> ("The Hawk in His Nest")

Historians love to talk about this serendipitous thing called destiny or fate. They suggest that the life of some exceptional individual sometimes magically coincides with the needs of a particular historical moment and culture. That person's talent and intelligence provide a sort of necessary mineral or amino acid to create change, or to ventilate the culture of an era.

In hindsight, we may call this process *destiny*, but our own experience tells us that any such transformation is a matter of enormous and prolonged effort. In fact, the coincidence in a single person of those two ingredients, will and inspiration, is a rare natural event. The world is full of people with lots of *inspiration*, but no will; these individuals remain perpetual dreamers or go into advertising. There are also many people with plentiful *will*, but no inspiration; they often go into the professions of world domination. But when these two qualities are aligned, the result can be an individual with rare presumption and intensity. That thing we call destiny is composed of thousands of *choices* that an individual makes, again and again, to keep going forward against resistance and into discovery. As Bly says in another of his poems from the period, "Hands developed with terrible labor by apes / Hang from the sleeves of evangelists."

It is easy to celebrate a great figure in a tone of elegy or nostalgia. The problem with such a perspective on the achievements of the past is that it is regretful and passive. Such regret acknowledges the loss of something valuable without igniting aspiration for the present and the future. In a time when we are encouraged to think of careers instead of souls, encouraged to be clever instead of speaking from the core of the self, Bly models an alternative path, a highly inconvenient yet considerably more heroic one.

T. S. Eliot—that father-figure poet whom the young Robert Bly never tired of mocking and denouncing—delivers some relevant lines in "East Coker." He says that "old men ought to be explorers." Bly's life, which can only be sketchily represented here, is an atlas of such journeys, quests, labor, and discovery. If old men ought to be such explorers, we might add, so should young men and young women.

"Who Wished to Improve Us
a Little by Living"
Remembering Auden's Influence

Of whom shall we speak? For every day they die
Among us, those who were doing us some good,
    And knew it was never enough but
    Hoped to improve a little by living.
    —from "In Memory of Sigmund Freud"

There was a time when every high school literature anthology contained Wystan Auden's poem, "The Unknown Citizen," for its ironical portrait of modern man's anonymous place in a bureaucratic world. "He was found by the Bureau of Statistics to be / One against whom there was no official complaint." Though it is not actually an outstanding example of Auden's work, the poem was nonetheless a perfectly pitched cultural document for the moment, a 1984-ish critique of the bureaucratic Orwellian state, in tune with both the Cold War and America's prosperous embrace of social conformity. Auden's poem was perfectly made for the soundbite of the classroom and professional intellectuals. Perhaps the poem unintentionally served as a preparation for the nonconformist Age of Aquarius. "Museé de Beaux Artes," "Lay Your Sleeping Head My Love," "As I Walked Out One Evening": these were a few of Auden's other greatest popular hits. For thirty-some years, Auden was as iconic a figurehead for poetry as Robert Frost. With his huge, exhausted, elephantine face, he carried an air of world-weary bemusement and gravitas perfect for a spokesperson for the "Age of Anxiety"—a phrase coined by Auden himself. He was, as well, a rhetorical wizard. In his youthful work of the 1930s, he roiled up the British literary world with enigmatic landscapes which contained an ominous ambience of Marxist social threat. In his later work, he seemed to channel Horace and Juvenal into Anglo-American modern poetics, and upheld the office of poet as social analyst.

Auden's star is slung much lower now—if not canonically, then popularly. Though in many ways the quintessential English poet of the twentieth century, one who gave poetic language its "modernist" flavor as much as Eliot—his poems are not much referenced by young poets now.

This disfavor is somewhat perplexing, because so many aspects of Auden's sensibility and talent would seem to suit contemporary taste so well: his bantering wit, his lexical wordplay and clashing of Latinate and Saxon dictions, his interest in elaborate poetic forms, his intensely figured surfaces, his sensitivity to the economic and social dimensions of human identity; they all make sense in the current climate of sensibility. Today's poetry zeitgeist is a gallery of highly mannered styles, epigrammatic wit, verbal and intellectual sophistication—all dimensions of Auden's extraordinary palette.

It's easy enough to detect an Audenesque presence in the work of contemporary hyperverbal poets like Matthea Harvey, Joshua Clover, or many others. Auden's ingenious affection for the polyglot plasticity of language, the rubbing together of public and private vocabularies, secular and sacred dictions, and his love of the declarative are now all widespread contemporary stylistic features. To illustrate the resemblance, here is an excerpt from Section XIV of Auden's poem "The Quest":

> Fresh addenda are published every day
> To the encyclopedia of the Way.
>
> Linguistic notes and scientific explanations,
> And texts for schools with modernized spelling and
>   illustrations.
>
> Now everyone knows the hero must choose the old horse,
> Abstain from liquor and sexual intercourse

And look out for a stranded fish to be kind to:
Now everyone thinks he could find, if he had a mind to,

The way through the waste to the chapel in the rock
For a vision of the Triple Rainbow or the Astral Clock.

And here's a stylistically similar passage from Matthea Harvey's poem, "Minarets and Pinnacles":

Around 5 o'clock even the grounded crowds
of aging coquettes who still believed the bat of an eyelash

or two could cause the miracle of upward mobility,
stood still, watching the tangerine streaks of sunset.

They did not remember why they did it.
Ties to God had proven fickle—first the prayermats

were put in the pantry in case the maid happened to upset
the olive oil & then the gold podiums seemed perfect

for those lengthy articles about real estate & roof repairs.

The quick declarative tone, the verbal charm of a narrator who is discoursing with an ear for sound and wit, the crisp, self-conscious use of public and private vocabularies which describe social life, the typifying intelligence, the comedy of manners—all of these manners seem Audenesque to me. Why then isn't Auden on more college reading lists, or commonly acknowledged as a contemporary mentor?

In fact, it is not Auden's sophistication or humor that seem irrelevant to the contemporary aesthetic: it's more probably the mature Auden's baseline of *rationality*; his penchant for sense-making, clarity, and his worn-on-the-sleeve humanism place him outside the zone of contemporary taste. Auden *cares* too much and too frankly about humanity, and he makes too much sense; he is too clear and crisp a thinker to appeal to an avant-garde sensibility. Digresser he is, but not an errant one, nor "elliptical" enough to be hip. The contemporary general disbelief in "truth," in the possibility of knowing, and our counter-faith in the instability of language and the unreliability of ideas all make Auden seem problematically "obvious."

It would be hard to know from contemporary poetics, but Auden's imprint can be found in the styles of dozens of American poets in the forties, fifties, and sixties; from Muriel Rukeyser to Louis MacNeice to Louis Simpson to Richard Wilbur. Seventy years ago, almost any poet drawn to the enterprise of "knowing"—any rhetorical poet, that is—would have been formatively steeped in Auden. Here, for example, is Anthony Hecht, sounding Auden-urbane in the beginning of his poem "Birdwatchers of America":

> It's all very well to dream of a dove that saves,
>   Picasso's or the Pope's,
> The one that annually coos in Our Lady's ear
>   Half the world's hopes,
> And the other one that shall cunningly engineer
> The retirement of all businessmen to their graves.

In a more hermetic, prophetic mode, Hecht's poem "Three Prompters from The Wings" echoes Auden's mannerism of abstract ironic moralism.

> Now today an old abuse
> Raises its head and festers
> To the scandal and disease
> Of all. He will weed it out
> And cleanse the earth of it.
> Clearly, if anyone could,
> He can redeem these lands;
> To doubt this would be absurd.

To glance through American poetry of the forties is to see how very pervasive Auden's influence was—often registered in a level of diction which is analytical and detached, yet peculiarly affectionate for the foibles it narrates. Howard Nemerov's well-respected ironic humanism was an adaptation of the urbane irony of the British poet. In his poem "A Day on the Big Branch," Nemerov describes a group of all-night gamblers at dawn, who decide

111

                                    to climb up to a place
one of us knew, with some vague view
of cutting losses or consolidating gains
by the old standard appeal to the wilderness,
the desert, the empty places of our exile,
bringing only the biblical bread and cheese
and cigarettes got from a grocer's on the way,
expecting to drink only the clear cold water
among the stones, and remember, or forget.

What does it mean to be Audenesque? One characteristic feature is the amalgamation of one diction with an incongruous other. Here, it is Audenesque to apply the financial idiom of stockbrokers ("cutting losses or consolidating gains") to the psychological; similarly, "the old standard appeal to the wilderness" seems quite Auden-ish, in its manner of characterizing the most venerable patterns of human community as old news, even while continuing to value them.

Virtually any American poet of the mid-century possessed of political intentions would have schooled themselves in the tone and diction of Auden to aim her or his arrows. It is a rhetorical style which joins together intellectual keenness with a tone of tired disillusioned humanity, while still preserving a smidgen of necessary hope.

Muriel Rukeyser, a poet of lifelong ardent social conscience, surely found a model in Auden's work for hectoring the great establishments. Although she learned to rough-up and compress the impeccable Continental smoothness of Auden-speak into American, Rukeyser never forsook Auden's didactic mode of declarative abstraction, and its resultant authority. Rukeyser probably was also nourished by Auden's stubborn propensity for faith, both revolutionary and spiritual.

You dynamiting the structure of our loves
embrace your lovers solving antithesis,
open your flesh, people, to opposites
conclude the bold configuration, finish
the counterpoint: sky, include earth now.

                                    ("Theory of Flight")

In Rukeyser one also finds Auden's youthful fondness for grand accusation, accusation so abstractly phrased that one is left feeling baffled but uneasy, convinced of the speaker's political sophistication, but clueless as to the exact occasion:

> In the human cities, never again to
> despise the backside of the city, the ghetto,
> or build it again as we build the despised
> backsides of houses.   Look at your own building.
> You are the city.

("Despisals")

Rukeyser herself has suffered the neglect of popular readership outside the classrooms of political feminism. She is found guilty of being too urgently sincere. Auden's sin, from a postmodern perspective, can be located in his belief in progress, or at least his faith in the essential nobility of effort in the human condition. Few poets have been as intelligent in typifying the big forces which drive us (nature, culture, law); but Auden actually believed such forces might be recognized, named, and made conscious. He insisted on acting *as if*—as if individual consciousness, however foolish and enmeshed, might fumble its way to certain recognitions, and thereby aspire to choice—that was his human hope. As the poet says in his great elegy for Sigmund Freud:

> If often he was wrong and at times absurd,
>> To us he is no more a person
>> Now but a whole climate of opinion
>
> Under whom we conduct our differing lives:
> Like weather he can only hinder or help,
>> The proud can still be proud but find it
>> A little harder, and the tyrant tries to
>
> To make him do but doesn't care for him much.

The legitimate criticism of Auden's poetry—his late poetry, that is—is that it is *too* conscious, too dominated by ideology, and not sufficiently complicated by the verbal peculiarity of the unconscious. Even Randall Jarrell, the greatest American mid-century critic and a fervent Auden admirer, found fault with the smooth ideological assuredness of the poet's later work—he found Auden's late work too rhetorically seamless, too subject to insights produced by rationality, no longer in touch with the unpredictable id.

"How conscious," asks Jarrell, "rational, controlled . . . can poetry afford to be? . . . I think one can safely say that Auden's later method is too conscious and controlled; too Socratic, too Alexandrian. . . . Poetry . . . represents the unconscious . . . as well as the conscious, our lives as well as our thoughts, and . . . has its true source in the first and not the second. . . . The sources of poetry . . . are not merely checked, but dried up, by too rigorous supervision. . . . We should distrust . . . any Rational . . . Method of Becoming a Saint."

Not surprisingly, it is through the work of John Ashbery that Auden's influence has been transmitted, in viral form, to the next generation: Ashbery's rhetorical free-flow and urbane, polytonal diction. Ashbery, while far less concerned about real sense-making than Auden, has the older poet's ability to conjure authoritative discourse in a broad variety of tones. Auden could write well on any topic. Ashbery retains all that discursive fluency, while dispensing with the issue of "topics." Thus, he was discovered and claimed a new poetic world for American poetry.

Here are some sentences, from Ashbery's early poem, "The Task" (the bland, abstract title itself is Audenesque) with its evocation of the heroic journey motif, full of Auden-like pronouncements and tones—formality, fluidity, and generality:

It is the blankness that follows gaiety, and Everyman must
    depart
Out there into stranded night, for his destiny
Is to return unfruitful out of the lightness
That passing time evokes. . . .

Yet if these are regrets they stir only lightly
The children playing after supper,
Promise of the pillow and so much in the night to come.

Ashbery's absurdism and non-sequitur, his temperamental refusal of resolution, are unlike Auden. But the declamatory, ranging authority rings familiar. If the critic Jarrell regretted Auden's loss of primal strangeness, what would he have made of Auden's irrational successor? He would have been surprised at an aesthetic future in which the unconscious essence of poetry would be drawn, not from an *individual* consciousness, but from a *culturally* collective cloud of scrambled rhetorics and idioms.

As for Auden—we need not weep for him. He would not be shocked at hearing the news that he is not much in fashion here at the beginning of the twenty-first century. He was fully initiated into the classical perspective on Fortuna. His work expresses a consistent, unbitter skepticism that anyone's reputation will endure. No one understood the vanities and errata of history and fame better than Auden: "The words of the dead are modified in the guts of the living," as he says in his elegy for William Butler Yeats. More often, they are simply shat out without digestion.

Nonetheless, like any great poet, Auden's body of work is full of undiscovered riches. His talent is immense. His work is a huge vein of ore still running through the Klondike of the English Language. If they knew to look, young poets might find a source-text in the early hermetic, sometimes sinister Auden. Consider the dark authoritative mystery of passages like this, from "The Question":

> To ask the hard question is simple:
> Asking at meeting
> With the simple glance of acquaintance
> To what these go
> And how these do;
> To ask the hard question is simple,
> The simple act of the confused will.
>
> But the answer
> Is hard and hard to remember: . . .
> And forgetting to listen or see
> Makes forgetting easy,
> Only remembering the method of remembering,
> Remembering only in another way,
> Only the strangely exciting lie,

Afraid
To remember what the fish ignored,
How the bird escaped, or if the sheep obeyed.

Till, losing memory,
Bird, fish, and sheep are ghostly,
And ghosts must do again
What gives them pain.
Cowardice cries
For windy skies,
Coldness for water,
Obedience for a master.

Jarrell, in discussing Auden, cites the deeply ingested influences of Freud, Darwin, Marx, and the Gospels; traces of the first two are visible in "The Question"; but even knowing that, this haunted, intense lyricism resembles nothing else in poetry. With his recurrent motifs of health and sickness as civic conditions, of folklore and myth as deep story-structures for human life, and his eccentric rich collation of paradigms, Auden has the deepest pockets intellectually of any modern poet.

From the start, from the poems he wrote in his twenties, everyone could see Auden's genius, even without entirely understanding the poems. Auden could make morality sound wearily, marvelously mature—rueful, outmoded, but finally the only alternative for the civilized person. That sagacious air is only one of his many distillations of modern consciousness. If his work can seem somewhat invulnerable in its assuredness, what has been commonly forgotten is the tenderness and pathos which often radiates from his discourse, like the poignant strangeness of this passage from "Easter":

Coming out of me living is always thinking,
Thinking changing and changing living,
Am feeling as it was seeing—
In city leaning on harbour parapet
To watch a colony of duck below
Sit, preen, and doze on buttresses
Or upright paddle on flickering stream,
Casually fishing at a passing straw.

Those find sun's luxury enough,
Shadow know not of homesick foreigner
Nor restlessness of intercepted growth.

There are many Audens to choose from, from the older, weary humanist to the uncannily intuitive early menacing savant. In his collected craft essays, *The Dyer's Hand*, Auden advises the serious young poet to find brilliant outlier models and mentors for her art; to find a secret poet from another historical time and place and marinate her talent in such freshness. It will serve as a sort of private treasure chest for one's own development. Now that Auden's own great and startlingly various poetry lies in a state of relative neglect, he seems like a perfect candidate for young poets to revisit, and undertake exactly the process he himself recommended.

The Poet as Wounded Citizen

About a year ago, on a late Tuesday afternoon, my therapist crossed his long, khaki-clad legs and said, "Well, no wonder you're feeling anxious and depressed. Look at the world: the terrible things that are happening, the political hypocrisy and greed, climate change, famine, mass shootings, it's terribly disturbing."

Sure, his explanation sounded good, and I was tempted to accept it. However, over time, I have observed that my therapist's methods of encouragement sometimes include flattery. More than once in that tiled studio office, with its cozy woodstove, skylight and giant tropical plants, I've been given credit for more wisdom than I actually possess. In fact, I'm much more self-centered than he imagines—I rarely pay attention to what is happening in the larger world. My self-preoccupation renders me too shortsighted to feel very deeply about Bangladesh, or the collapse of the Portuguese economy. My therapist extends me too much credit if he imagines that my inner life is some kind of seismographic meter tuned to the planetary wavelengths.

The equation of one's personal unease with the illness of the world can easily have the appearance of melodrama, grandiosity, or narcissism. But then again, self-inflation may well be the necessary price of real artistic ambition.

In his great poem "America," Allen Ginsberg correlates his neurosis with the country's own nationalistic paranoia:

> I'd better consider my national resources.
> My national resources consist of two joints of marijuana
>   millions of genitals an unpublishable private literature
>   that jetplanes 1400 miles an hour and twentyfive-thousand
>   mental institutions.

> I say nothing about my prisons nor the millions of
>> underprivileged who live in my flowerpots under the light
>> of five hundred suns.

On the one hand, Ginsberg's poem resembles a paranoiac fugue state; on the other, his disrobing of America is darkly passionately and painfully astute. It is one of many remarkable features of this great twentieth-century poem that in its conclusion, the speaker transmutes his personal grief, anger, and mania into an affirmative pledge to improve the collective future. "I am America" he says; and "I'm putting my queer shoulder to the wheel."

Is the citizen-artist really a microcosm of the society to which she belongs? The shopworn analogy that has been used in the past for this hard-to-define civic function of art is the comparison of the artist to a canary in the coal mine. In the early nineteen hundreds, the canary was used as a kind of carbon monoxide detector for underground workers. When the canary stops singing and is found in a little heap of feathers at the bottom of its cage, that's when the coal miners know that it is time to get out of the mine, or to improve the air quality. To follow this analogy, when its poets stop singing—or when they start jumping off bridges—it is an indication that a civilization is in trouble.

In her critical study, *The End of the Novel of Love*, the essayist Vivian Gornick compares the culturally crucial artist not to a canary but to a set of prescient fingertips. "In great novels," she says, "we always feel that the writer, at the time of the writing, . . . is struggling to make sense of what is perceived somewhere in the nerve endings, if not yet in clarified consciousness."

As Gornick suggests, it is not that the writer sees what no one else can. The artist is not a freak or an oracle or a genius. In fact, the artist is at the epicenter of normality. Poets are wounded in the same ways as everyone else, but with one particular distinction—they are not wounded to the point of *speechlessness*. Instead, they are wounded *into* speech. Their job, unlike the roles assigned to most of us, is not to conceal or to disguise their woundedness, but to make it glaringly evident. Poets are useful to the culture precisely to the extent that their experience is representative—representative, and murderously frank. With the precision and frankness that is cultivated by poetic craft, the poet might be one whose complaint can trigger widespread recognitions.

Here is the beginning of "Poem," by Muriel Rukeyser written in the seventies:

> I lived in the first century of world wars.
> Most mornings I would be more or less insane,
> The newspapers would arrive with their careless stories,
> The news would pour out of various devices
> Interrupted by attempts to sell products to the unseen.
> I would call my friends on other devices;
> They would be more or less mad for similar reasons.

The poet is a citizen with a complaint, but it would probably be a mistake to assume that what the poet has to say is commercially *useful* in any obvious way. Is Sylvia Plath's poem "Daddy" for example, with its notorious, hyperbolic comparison of the speaker's father to a Nazi storm trooper, *useful?* Is it *useful* for the poet to say "Every woman adores a Nazi"? The poem is not notable for its diplomacy, its sense of proportion, or its lucid rationality. If the report offered by a poem *is* useful, it is valuable for its personalization, the intensity with which it bears down, even irrationally, on every part of the world. And that is the gist of it, finally; the world *needs* personalizing. That is part of poetry's job, in our time more than ever.

This is why we should be wary if our poets and artists grow too humble, or timid, or circumscribed in their sense of their own authority; too modest, serene, or lovey-dovey. Oddly enough, their woundedness has to be honored, encouraged, even protected. The danger to the poet is not limitation itself, but that she or he might lose touch with the world, and the human condition.

"If we are at war, why aren't we suffering?" asked a writer friend of mine, sitting at a restaurant table, one evening, a winter or two ago—so simple, so naïve, that question, yet it just hangs there in the air, waiting to be answered. I can hear her say it more loudly: "If "we" are at *war*, why aren't "we" suffering?!" A few heads turned from the direction of nearby tables, then looked away again, embarrassed. What empowers poetry is the need of the wounded to talk about his or her inconvenient and irritating wound, which is by proxy everyone's.

The American poet James Tate started as an artful, quirky, and twitchy personality-poet. Over many decades, however, his work evolved beyond the boundaries of personal neurosis, into the comic testimonies of a baffled, isolated, and frightened Everyman. Tate's poem "Bounden Duty" seems, in its way, like a postmodern reprise of Auden's well known political poem from another era, "The Unknown Citizen." This dramatic monologue expresses the speaker's paranoid suspicion of what passes for normal, a comic estrangement from the surfaces of daily life that seems very familiar, and contemporary:

> I got a call from the White House, from the
> President himself, asking me if I'd do him a personal
> favor. I like the President, so I said, "Sure, Mr.
> President, anything you like." He said, "Just act
> like nothing's going on. Act normal. That would
> mean the world to me. Can you do that, Leon?" "Why
> sure, Mr. President, you've got it. Normal, that's
> how I'm going to act. I won't let on, even if I'm
> tortured," I said, immediately regretting that "tortured"
> bit. He thanked me several times and hung up. I was
> dying to tell someone that the President himself called
> me, but I knew I couldn't. The sudden pressure to
> act normal was killing me. And what was going on
> anyway. I didn't know anything was going on. I
> saw the President on TV yesterday. He was shaking
> hands with a farmer. What if it wasn't really a
> farmer? I needed to buy some milk, but suddenly
> I was afraid to go out. I checked what I had on.
> I looked "normal" to me, but maybe I looked more
> like I was trying to be normal. That's pretty
> suspicious. I opened the door and looked around.
> What was going on?

In "Bounden Duty" we feel the speaker's sense of inner woundedness, his ennui and powerlessness; all symptoms of the utter loss of perspective which is so much a part of modern sensibility. We may call it normal, and accept it as normal, but the poem infers, with the eloquence of paranoia, that it is not. Distortion, and a loss of proportion are the symptoms of the American citizen. The speaker's psychosis might be merely comic if it were merely personal, but because Tate unfolds the narrative with pitch-perfect tone we understand it as a representation of universal dislocation.

More than ever, the function of the wounded poet is relevant to us now, in the twenty-first century, when we are experiencing more transformation, voluntary and involuntary, than ever before. We live in a time, an era and a place which seems designed to drown wakefulness in hypnotic superabundance. The hyperactive striving and distraction generated by contemporary information is marvelously effective at obscuring our awareness of our own estrangement. Media surfeit, infinitely addictive consumerism, and lack of proportion are our carbon monoxide—maybe we are the canaries dying from the fumes of Facebook. The amazing adroitness of our technological disassociations, and of political and commercial misrepresentation, are, sorry to say, the supreme human achievement of our time.

The poet's pestering, plaintive reminder that alienation and disconnection are real and urgently significant forms of suffering is important. It is the artist's function to remind us that to be disconnected from your own biology and emotional life is an authentic kind of pain. Our age, with its endlessly sophisticated trash, expects us to eat junk food and say thank you. The wounded poet, suffering from indigestion, may remind us that to eat such shit ultimately is an insult to our humanity. As Tomas Tranströmer says in the end of his poem, "Streets in Shanghai," "We all look so happy out here in the sunlight; but each of us is dying from a wound he knows nothing about."

In her poem "Responding," the poet Juliana Spahr expresses the same distress in a slightly more postmodern, but no less canny manner. Her assertion is simple: that our political environment is intimately connected to our emotional and mental health, or lack of it. To take the risk of feeling that connection is to be driven towards more, perhaps even more unbearable exploration, and perhaps to begin to voice the protest that requires change:

> This is a place without a terrain a government that always
>   changes an unstable language. Even buildings disappear
>   from day to day. . . .

> the condition of unbearableness is the constant state of
>   mind for all occupants

> we read all day in the village square during the rule of
>   [name of major historical figure] a book that is so subtle

>   [its political content goes unnoticed

> what is political content?

Poets must continue to live close to the wound, and poems to speak from the edge of what the culture at large is unwilling to know. And quite possibly, they need to shriek at the top of their lungs, and even to exaggerate. *What is this feeling I feel?*, we ask. What is the name of this dis-ease? What word for this breathless, speedy, anxious feeling of barely being able to bear this psychotic and trashy man-made world? What is its cause, and what might be its cure? When we ask these kinds of seemingly naïve questions, and ask them loud, it may be we are standing up in protest to articulate the ailment—not just our own, but everyone's.

Mass Culture and the American Poet
The Poem as Vaccination

I once drove around southwest Arizona with a photographer named Pedro from Mexico City. His specialty was making ethnographic forays into North America, and on this trip he was studying the culture of RVs—recreational vehicles—and their owners. In the American Southwest especially, these colonies of mobile homes are a common sight. Their migrant inhabitants are mostly older couples, American retirees who drive south for the winter, north for the summer—they rotate between Michigan, say, and New Mexico, or between Maine and Florida. Higher incomed Americans often have two real homes; but these less-affluent migrants winter in places like Yuma, Arizona, which is where we were.

A standard American recreational vehicle is roughly the size of a railroad boxcar. They have kitchens and beds and bathrooms, satellite TV dishes, flower boxes on their window sills; their exteriors are personalized with slogans and airbrushed paintings of elk. My Mexican photographer friend took hundreds of photographs of these vehicles and their people; deeply suntanned, pot-bellied old men walking little dogs. Women chatting over collapsible fences between their vehicles, like neighbors in a Norman Rockwell painting. This is what Pedro said about his subjects: "Of all the North Americans I have seen," he said, "these ones have most fully realized the American dream—to live *inside* an appliance."

It was easy enough to make fun of those people. Their RVs had brand names like Voyager, Windsong, Open Road, or Apache. They lived in child-free temporary "parks," which were really parking lots, with hookups for electricity and water. But it's also possible to see them as legitimate American dreamers, exemplars of the pioneer spirit, restless non-conformists in their covered wagons, agents of self-sufficiency roaming over the land. These nomads have found a solution to an identity problem; they have both the containment which a human nature requires to know itself, and they have the freedom to remain unconfined, to change their circumstances at will. Thus, they can medicate both the conditions of claustrophobia and agoraphobia at once. One could say that the RV nomad life is a way of living inside the very belly of the beast, but refusing to be digested. I wonder, how much better can an American poet do?

The ill effects and anonymity of mass culture are so well known, and have been so well-described in literature and social analysis that even to bring them up can seem tiresome. We take them for granted. Isn't this news already a hundred years old? And wasn't it, back then, poetically well-articulated by T. S. Eliot, William Carlos Williams, and E. E. Cummings ? Hasn't this modern lament been already thoroughly sung? To complain about advertising for new cars and antidepressants seems touchingly naïve. One feels like a cliché from the 1950s, warning that the invention of television is going to make us into communists.

In this essay however, I want to claim that mass culture, far from being a dead subject, is an ongoing challenge for poetry, one that remains complex and demanding of all our artistic ingenuity and confrontational resources.

The symptoms of our commercialized environment are familiar—a loss of fundamental contact with reality, an inability to think and feel clearly, a sense of proportion that is relentlessly invaded, destabilized, and distorted. The end result is a sense of being both magnificently stimulated and trivialized, and an anesthetized condition of self that is, paradoxically, a radical kind of suffering. The problem we have inherited is a permanent one: how is it possible for the American poet to grapple with these aspects of mass culture, whose mind-bending presence is equal to any event in our private lives? How is it possible to include the marketplace in our report on the world, without being engulfed by it? Is irony sufficient? Will aloof superiority serve well enough?

Many ingenious poetic strategies have been marshaled in the

twentieth century to engage mass culture, but Mark Halliday's smart, discursive poem, "Seventh Avenue," models an approach admirable for its succinct formulations. "Romance hates democracy" the poet says, and, "How can I be golden inside / when there are so many like me? / it's loud enough already," he says.

Late Tuesday afternoon the romantic self weaves
up Seventh Avenue amid too many lookers, too many
feelers: romance hates democracy;

how can *you* be so great and golden inside
if your trunk is shouldered among other trunks
block after block, block after block—

It's loud enough already

out here on Seventh Avenue with that cat's boom box
and these three giggle girls being Madonna together
and that guy hawking wind-up titans wielding laser lances.

Who's Wordsworth for any extended period on Seventh Ave?
In this pre-dusk traffic you catch the hint
that Manuel and thou if seers at all are seers only

for seconds—now the steak, taxi, buttocks, headline
and wallet resume their charismatic claim to be what counts.
Soul on Seventh is a sometime on-off quick-flip thing . . .

What I want is a poem long as Seventh Avenue
to sprinkle gold on every oppressed minority,
every young woman's subtly female hips,
every sad and suspicious American face
and the quiddity of every mud-tracked pizza shop;
proving, block after block, stanza by stanza,
that I'm not just one skinny nervous pedestrian
but the one who matters because he sees and says.
I want that. The Avenue grins and says
"You want that? How does it feel to want?"

"Seventh Avenue" lucidly identifies one central conundrum of mass culture—the ways in which it makes our environment rich, desirable, and diverse, a place where we encounter "that cat's boom box / and these three giggle girls being Madonna together," where pizza shops and street vendors of different social classes and colors are part of the inextricable sensorium of the American Real, self-evident in their necessity and value. In some sense, we need and crave and love all this hullabaloo.

At the same time Halliday's speaker protests against the way that multiplicity blurs the definitions of experience, how it destroys the boundaries of the self without necessarily offering in exchange a valuable experience of communion. The idealized experience the speaker longs for in "Seventh Avenue" is the oceanic vision of Whitman, who could encompass multitudes without destroying their (or his own) distinctness. In "Seventh Avenue," however, instead of Whitmanian connectedness, the speaker has the experience of being swallowed and diminished.

It's sometimes been suggested that the challenge for contemporary poetry is to try harder, to compete more effectively for attention in the marketplace; but that idea is so ill-conceived it is hardly even worth calling wrong. The real story of poetic modernism is the story of the twentieth century itself. As so many value systems and ideologies collapsed in the twentieth century—divine order, faith in progress, the veneration of family and ancestors, and belief in human nature itself—poetry's cultural authority also shrank and was destabilized. Poetry's share of the general disintegration was loss of power, and loss of an audience that looked to it to dispense wisdom and value. Its claim to transcendental vision was disenfranchised. The heavy oak podium from which the (yes, white male) poets sang and declaimed their poems was crated up and stored in the dank church basement. Then the church was bulldozed.

In that sense, contemporary poetry's preoccupation with individual emotional identity and narrative is a kind of compensatory shift, a revised business plan; its relocation to the realm of personal psychology—via confessionalism, for instance—is how American poetry has maintained a claim to usefulness. Often it seems that poetry's last, viable position has become the realm of the psychological; i.e., the defense of the one non-commercial property that remains our own—the private self. To state this more optimistically, if poetry can no longer affect a whole culture, it can nonetheless reach one person at a time.

Another strategic dimension of "Seventh Avenue" is how Halliday's speaker does not disguise or omit the concerns of his own insecure selfishness from the poem. If this adds a comedic dimension to the speaker's complaint, and thus perhaps risks a kind of anti-romantic self-deprecation, it also acknowledges a complexity of poignant, even tragic dimension—how the beauty of selfhood is hindered by the competing equalities of other people. Spoken by the impure instrument of the speaker's *personality*, the poem defends the somewhat shabby romantic self even while acknowledging its modernity-damaged condition. "Romance hates democracy," he says—and that statement resonates with enough truth-telling gravitas to hold our attention.

Halliday's clear-headed presentation showcases one example of how a contemporary poet can undogmatically formulate and confront the complex challenge of mass culture and human otherhoods, without denying its sexy charismatic dazzle, nor over-simplifying the real danger of the individual being overwhelmed, contaminated, or destroyed by such reality. It's a poem that combines seriousness, élan, convincing quirkiness, and a lasting coherence.

The Poem as Laboratory Experiment

Artistically, as well as existentially, we might as well give our great steroidal culture demon a proper name, and let that name be *Surfeit*. For the artist, on a sheerly technical level, that surfeit presents a bona fide problem of volume and velocity. It is difficult for a poem, or a reader, to drink from a wide open, blasting firehose. A poet needs to allow enough culture—call it raw data—into the poem to provide a credible database. Only then might she perform a kind of analytical dissection of it. In the mere activity of cataloguing American variety and spectacle, the available stories and tones of contemporary culture, a kind of intoxication with abundance can easily set in, an imitative excess like that found in over-crowded poetic passages, like "Double Album" by Scott Ruescher:

> Even if a European pilgrim, from the crazed Elvis festivals
> Of Belgium and Holland, had been waiting to perform

A medley of the ballads on acoustic guitar for me
In the doorway of the Greyhound station the day I left town,
Or if the so-called "scoremaster" on the *Naked Elvis* quiz show
Had removed an item of clothing between each round of the
   game
Until he was naked, right out there on the live show
That I've finally managed to watch on British television;

If those Japanese hipsters from *Mystery Train*,
The Jim Jarmusch film from the 1980s, had shown up to do
Their heavily accented but convincing imitation
Of Elvis rehearsing in front of a hotel mirror . . .
In the lobby of the fleabag hotel where Screamin' Jay
   Hawkins,
Playing the part of the night clerk with such natural
   panache,
Put such a spell on me with his method-free acting
That I never again confused him with Lightning Hopkins . . .

"Double Album" is a well-written, energetic poem that illustrates the potential hazard of engaging with mass culture, in all
its flashy, crazy surfeit. Reading it is like watching a lion tamer
be seized, dragged into the bush, and eaten by his own lion—the
poet swallowed by his own subject matter. On evidence of these
opening sixteen lines, there seems little likelihood of the poet
regaining control of his creation.

A skillful poem of surfeit, yes, must allow enough data in to
convincingly represent the world. But it also has to be able to
shut the valve, pause, and resist, for the sake of self-preservation.
In this way the topical poem can be viewed as a kind of science
project, which honestly allows all the variables of the outer world
into its laboratory, but limits the sample size in order to perform
its analysis. The outcome of the game must not be rigged, but it
must be overseen, and orchestrated.

To put it in a more proactive way, let us ask: Can the poem
function as a working model for negotiating our problem at
large, instructing us in how to encounter the real, while at the
same time protecting us?

If Mark Halliday's poem is outspoken and discursive, Linda Gregg's poem "Growing Up" offers another model of poetic strategy in handling mass culture. By contrast, Gregg's narrative monologue operates almost entirely on levels of understatement and implication. Here too, the desire of the speaker for the larger world is real. Here too, the existence of other people is a problem.

Gregg's protagonist features a single woman, alone at home, at night, doing two things at once: reading a book while also watching a story on television with the sound off. The movie— "I've seen [it] before," she says—is one whose romantic plot is obvious and familiar. The protagonist-speaker is represented as a casualty of that great merchandising scheme, the myth of romantic love. Here is the entire poem:

> I am reading Li Po. The TV is on
> with the sound off.
> I've seen this movie before.
> I turn on the sound just for a moment
> when the man says, "I love you."
> Then turn it off and go on reading.

It's the psychological doubleness, the split of self here, that makes Gregg's poem poignant and penetrating. On the one hand, she finds the old romantic love still somewhat irresistible. She picks up the remote control and turns the sound on at the exact moment that the onscreen man says the word *love*. At the poem's end, nonetheless, we see the speaker "turn off" the romantic movie, and return to reading her volume of ancient Chinese poetry. Her interiority seems ultimately intact—though it will, probably, we also understand, never be fully restored to its previous state of wholeness.

Gregg's poem delivers an elegant vignette of what we are calling cultural self-vaccination. We watch the speaker "yield" to the temptation offered by the media, yet she also retains her instinct for self-possession. If she is somewhat stuck to, or wounded by, past history, she is also depicted as a strong individual. In this poem, for a moment at least, mass culture seems like a treatable condition, treatable by caution as well as interest. Gregg's reading material—classical Chinese poetry—additionally suggests ways in which art and historical knowledge are resources which can add ballast and equilibrium to a life.

What Gregg's poem is able to do is what poetry has been always valued for: to distill, localize, and intensify crucial aspects of the collective human experience. In the cross-currents of this understated but complex moment, the struggle of the poem's character is the struggle towards a viable position, not just in terms of personal psychology, but in terms of cultural stance. Her poem models the complex dialectic of participation in and aloofness from mass culture: first, to allow the entrance of a certain amount of cultural data, then how to practice skillful engagement with it.

The struggle of the individual with mass culture is a daunting, epic, ongoing battle—it is even mythological; one only has to think of Odysseus and his sirens. It might be tempting for a poet to steer past such seemingly familiar, already well-handled subject matter, foreseeing the many ways in which one will probably fail in the undertaking: the temptation of easy intellectual superiority, for example. But the obligation of poets to take on the fight is undiminished, as real as the struggle to retain selfhood in our daily lives. Artists are hardly superior in this struggle with surfeit; rather, to acknowledge and enact ("act out") the struggle in the open, on the page or canvas is a profoundly political function of art. Such poetry as we must teach ourselves to write will take cunning and inspiration, effort, artful invention, introspection and, in fact, an ever-evolving sophistication—all the myriad resources of great poetry.

The Wild Life of Metaphor

Prehensile, Triangulating, Insubordinate

> Each venture is a new beginning, a raid
> on the inarticulate with shabby equipment
> always deteriorating in the general mess of
> imprecision of feeling.
> —T. S. Eliot

> Nobody knows what a poem is.
> —Katie Condon

Poetics is the attempt to systematically describe what poetry is, or to taxonomize what happens in poems. It is an endlessly rewarding enterprise because poetry itself is so rich and various. Thus, no poetics ever entirely succeeds in comprehension. The critic Frank Kermode says that a great, real poem contains a "hermeneutical radiance" that endures, evades, and outlasts any analysis. That is why the essence of a poem can never be more than temporarily grasped by mere interpretation or diagram, and why we feel compelled to return over and over to good and great poems—there is something hidden, spring-loaded inside them that we cannot quite retain, that will not be possessed. You have to go back and revisit the source again, to fetch its essence. It won't stay "got." Of all the devices and elements of poetry, metaphor is one of the most unknowable, a protean phenomenon that can never be subordinated or fully defined, because it is a whole wilderness of things. The single term "metaphor"— we behave as if we know what the word means—is not remotely adequate to encompass the variety of ways in which consciousness uses figurative language to think and feel. In fact, every definition of metaphor fails when set against the spectrum of its employments. And yet, we keep studying, and helplessly trying to name its powers—as this essay does—for the sake of our own illumination.

Prehensile

For example: not long ago I was sitting on one side of a concert hall, watching three musicians set up their instruments. They wore traditional Indian costumes—shiny gold and embroidered gilt-colored gown-like pants and shirts—part of the gestalt of playing Indian music. Each of them settled onto a round cushion, cross-legged, using another cushion designed to support one knee.

And then, with no formal demarcation, while the audience was still being seated, it seemed, the music started. Without even looking up to see if anyone was paying attention, the tabla player had begun his quick, flutter-fingered percussive pitty-pat—tikky-tack, like light rain falling on cardboard; the pattern seemed to spread out like a puddle or a pool, and gradually infiltrate the room.

Then the ringing steel strings of the sitar begin to chime and whine, like a long sword sliding in and out of a pewter sheath, making angular diagonal strokes across the patterning of the tabla. Then all the instruments seem to gather, and advance, with great casualness, like a shifting fog seeping through the air conditioning vents, or like an animal, beginning to amble, then trot, then gallop. The music seemed to be like the shifting dappled spots on the back of a leopard moving through sunlight and shade; it had the quality of a collective entity.

As the preceding passage may suggest, the process of metaphor-making often resembles an act of reaching out, a kind of fumbling or tactile seeking. In his essay, "What the Image Can Do," Robert Bly coins the term *prehensile metaphor*, to describe this stretching forth in the attempt to grasp and bring back something. As we use it in life, in conversation and thought, this mode of metaphor is probably fundamental to thinking. Analogy is a kind of tentacle, seeking an image for something that we don't have a name for, seeking a way to formulate, to speak about or describe, to touch the experience. Metaphor-making in this style doesn't know exactly what it is "looking" for, or whether it will find it. It has an organic, creaturely quality, an elastic adroitness at stretching and grasping, and fetching back.

We can observe this prehensile stretching of metaphor in action in Gerald Stern's poem "I Remember Galileo":

> I remember Galileo describing the mind
> as a piece of paper blown around by the wind,
> and I loved the sight of it sticking to a tree
> or jumping into the back seat of a car,
> and for years I watched paper leap through my cities;
> but yesterday I saw the mind was a squirrel caught crossing
> Route 80 between the wheels of a giant truck,
> dancing back and forth like a thin leaf,
> or a frightened string, for only two seconds living
> on the white concrete before he got away,
> his life shortened by all that terror, his head
> jerking, his yellow teeth ground down to dust. . . .
>
> Paper will do in theory, when there is time
> to sit back in a metal chair and study shadows;
> but for this life I need a squirrel . . .

Stern is rather radically revising Galileo's image for the human mind, from an image emphasizing its whimsical random movement, to an image that connotes terror, flight, and endangerment. But his metaphor seems to be evolving and moving as it comes to us, as though he is stumbling on an idea that still has room to grow, or an idea that is preceding haphazardly and might recede again as it is tested, like the indecisive squirrel itself. The poet's restless, imaginative seeking for the comparison displays the wildly resourceful elasticity of our thirst to describe experience.

Triangulating Metaphor

We commonly tend to think of the relationship between a phenomenon and a corresponding metaphor as a singular one-to-one equation: "It was as difficult as eating spaghetti with your elbows," we say. Or, "He looked at me like an undertaker measuring a coffin." We often presume that one metaphor—the right one—will perform the job of concrete clarification. The right metaphor, we think, should clarify and settle the matter.

However, what if one image will not suffice? What if an experience, or feeling, or phenomenon is outside the range of conventional label, resistant to easy definition, so elusive that one image serves to be only a partial impression, only a fragmentary glimpse of the thing itself? What if the emotion or sensation you are trying to describe is deeply, paradoxically "mixed," or what if the reality of a situation has many contradictory sides to it?

In that case, a poet might employ multiple, sequential images meant to represent the elusive reality from different sides. This method could be called the method of metaphorical triangulation. Stevens's "Thirteen Ways of Looking at a Blackbird" is the canonical example of such a method. Denise Levertov's remarkable poem "The Mutes" is an even more concentrated performance.

In "The Mutes," we watch the speaker attempt to find an equation for the sexually suggestive vocalizations men make in public places about passing women. Contemporary culture may have settled on the general label of "harassment" for this phenomenon, but that label is a sociological category, not a vivifying—nor a curious—designation; Levertov's poem attempts to look beneath the obvious surface to the deeper and stranger actuality.

Levertov, however, takes her mission of description seriously, and finds a simple one-to-one verbal equation difficult, no, impossible to make. What we see on display in "The Mutes" is a powerful creative imagination engaged in true inquiry, trying on one notion after another as she attempts to name what these coarse noises truly are. Here is the opening of "The Mutes":

> Those groans men use
> passing a woman on the street
> or on the steps of the subway

to tell her she is a female
and their flesh knows it,

are they a sort of tune,
an ugly enough song, sung
by a bird with a slit tongue

but meant for music?

Or are they the muffled roaring
of deafmutes trapped in a building that is
slowly filled with smoke?

Perhaps both.

What are those noises? asks the poet. Are they a primal "tune"? If
so, she says, it is an ugly tune. Is it a song of some kind? If so,
she says, it is sung by an injured bird, but one with a suggestive
tongue.

On the other hand, says the poet, perhaps this noise is a
wounded, inarticulate cry for help, the noise a creature might
make who has no true speech of its own—a noise "sung" by men
whose nature is to be deaf and mute, who are trapped in themselves like people in a burning building? And what an image for
the suffering of lust that is!

Levertov goes on in her description, through other formulations for and evaluations of men who make these noises—but we
can observe from these lines that she is using metaphor as a kind
of enclosure in progress, a series of prodding triangulations attempting to locate the actual thing without "fixing" it, without
crucifying it on the cross of one single, simplifying noun. Male
lust is all of these things, the speaker suggests—brutal, aggressive, tragic, wounded, helpless, pitiable.

Just the spectacle of a writer grasping, and grasping again at a
reality, with such persistence and integrity, can be inspirational.
We see this act of metaphorical triangulation in Rilke's poem
"I live my life in growing orbits," (translated by Robert Bly) in
which the speaker is trying to describe the unnamable effort of
his inner life, what a new-age person would call his soul-life:

I live my life in growing orbits
which move out over the things of the world.
Perhaps I can never achieve the last,
but that will be my attempt.

I am circling around God, around the ancient tower,
and I have been circling for a thousand years,
and I still don't know if I am a falcon, or a storm,
or a great song.

Rilke is more romantic than Levertov, but, like her effort to define male lust, Rilke's effort is also, in some way, analytical. Rilke's heroic speaker claims not to know what he is—he is describing, after all, the pure mystery of human identity, a blank space, for which there is no name. "Who or what am I?" His initial construction is negative: "I still don't know." Yet in fact we can see that the speaker is claiming to share a resemblance to all three of these named phenomena, these nouns—he is like a falcon, he is like a storm, he is like a great song. The connotation of each is different—creature of flight, cluster of chaos, melodic performance—yet these images triangulate, and in their multiple, intersecting collaboration, they suggest the deep, alloyed core of the speaker with some accuracy.

Insubordinate Metaphor

If Levertov's metaphors in "The Mutes" suggest the rigorous analytical focus that metaphor can exert upon phenomena, the opposite is also true: images and metaphors often erupt from the subconscious with no apparent agenda. One of the most thrilling and addictive rewards of reading or writing poetry is the unexpectedness of what "surfaces," and such eruptions can be as much a surprise to the writer as the reader. The unpredictability of such images was the main goal of the French surrealist poets, but long before their modern aesthetic movement, the veneration of inscrutable divinatory speech "from somewhere else" was part of many cultures and societies: the Delphic Oracle in ancient Greece, the shamanic priests of the Inuit, the coded epigrams of the I Ching—all are valued for their shadowy origin, and their unsettling, urgent strangeness.

Such insubordinations of language and imagination are not always convenient. When metaphorical images erupt in this manner, they can overturn the orderly progression of the poem they belong to; they detour and distort, and they can startle us with their unexpected knowledge. Joanne Dominique Dwyer's poem "Shallow Person" (not yet published) sets off on one kind of journey, a speculative litany of self-exploration, both comical and serious:

> What if I were not a shallow person.
> What if I did not need honey in my mouth.
> What if I did not need an Arapaho blanket swaddled
> around me in order to sleep less fitfully.
> What if Caspian tigers were not extinct.
> What if we were all made of light . . .
> What if your dog bit you in the femoral artery
> while you were teaching your child to ride a bike.

Halfway through Dwyer's poem, however, an extended metaphor of an entirely different sort suddenly appears:

> What if the African continent lifted up from the earth
> and travelled like a magic carpet and landed on North
>   America
> smothering the USA as if it were putting out a fire
> and the African continent liked its new home
> and did not mind being a continent on top of another
>   continent,
> did not mind hearing all the dead below it crying
> out for ribs and coleslaw and beer.
> Others moaning for tofu and kale smoothies
> with a scoop of flax and whey.

Wow. Here the poem has jumped its tracks, and this image of the African continent "smothering" North America seems to be a sudden attack on American First-World privilege. Although it is not entirely unrelated to the wandering, self-inspecting agenda of the "Shallow Person" section, it is abrupt, stranger, more

138

political—and even more extended in its imaginative development than other units of the poem. It is like, let us say, a volcano sprouting up in the middle of a cornfield. The insubordinate imagination pushes its way into the frame with its unexpected news—highly political news—from the unconscious, and, in the middle of a personal poem, it brings tidings, at once brilliantly compressed and expansive, from the violent, scrambled unconsciousness of the modern world. Here, metaphor is Noam Chomsky on acid.

Looking Over the Brink of Metaphor

As we recognize the fluent, elastic, and multiplicitous nature of metaphor, especially as it occurs in poetry, as we grow more awake to its many manifestations, we might arrive at new levels of insight, perspectives which might even be compared to a spiritual revelation. Call it being inducted into the guild of metaphor. The first benefit of metaphorical initiation is the potential for a kind of psychic freedom. To perceive, after all, that the linguistic-imagistic universe is liquid, that it floats in a state of continuously permutating potential, is to feel that it is yours to make what you can of it. And this intuition—that human consciousness has access to the transformations of the verbal imagination—is a kind of secret superpower. The freedom of metaphor can make a dying man laugh and an orphaned child dance. In the pulsations of making and remaking images and sentences, we feel our visionary muscle touch and weave together with the roots of humor, archetype, myth, and narrative. Paradoxically, we are granted the ability not just to extract truth from the world, but to escape pure rationality, which can itself be a great empowerment.

Perhaps there is even a further recognition to be had from the way metaphor works: something about the raw, malleable nature of reality itself. Sometimes one might even glimpse reality's ultimate lack of substance. The Hindu concept of maya asserts that the world is a realm of a million changing appearances which seduce us endlessly into a kind of dance. Similarly, the Buddhist doctrine describes the world as unfixed, an endless parade of transitional forms which float on the surface of a profound unity. The serpentine figurations of metaphor-in-process are not much different.

Archetypes and parables of this fundamental truth of the world's plasticity circulate around us perpetually. In Book Four of Homer's *Odyssey*, the Greek chieftain Menelaus needs to know why his ships are becalmed. He is told that he must capture the Greek sea-god Proteus and force the deity to tell him the truth. Through cunning, Menelaus manages to seize Proteus and hold him as he changes form again and again, from lion to pig to serpent to tree to water—until finally, exhausted, the god yields, and tells Menelaus what he wishes to know. You must sacrifice three bulls, says Proteus, and say these prayers. Then the wind will carry you elsewhere.

But the story of Proteus is itself a metaphor for the nature of metaphor, metaphor that can change anything into anything. Its powers are manifold, elusive, and hard to control or hold onto. Proteus changes and changes. We watch, we play with metaphor, sometimes we use it fortunately and it empowers us; sometimes it defeats us. We grip Proteus in our fist and try to make him hold still. Gripped in the fist of the world, we ourselves periodically find that we can no longer change shape.

Proteus, the sea-god, is a shapeshifter, like water, and language is also in a sense water, always churning and transforming. Metaphor is one of the most remarkable deities of language, and we find out, in our occasional lucky freedom, that if we cannot command the god, he nonetheless mysteriously appears at our side. Perhaps with the right prayer, we can even enlist him to our cause. Before we let him go again, before he reverts to his formless origins, and the wind carries us elsewhere.

Poetry, the Dangers of Realism, and the Revisionist Power of Fantasy

The Shadow Side of Realism Is Fatalism

Last year at a conference, I listened to a well-respected speaker, one connected with a British ecological movement, commence his talk by saying that ecological climate disaster was inevitable. Not is it only inevitable, he told the audience, it already has happened. We are living in the shadow of a blast that has already occurred, an explosion whose effects we simply haven't felt yet.

The transatlantic flight that had brought him to the States, he reported, had left twenty tons of carbon in the earth's stratosphere. The car that had driven him from the airport had added more poison to the air. The birch and pine trees alongside the highway had the yellowish complexion of a kind of plant leukemia. The fish swimming through the waters of the local bays and rivers were being born blind, with anatomically misplaced sexual organs, due to the pharmaceutical sewage flushed from the cities and towns.

The guest speaker's report was dire. His audience—the kind that attends such talks—was the kind that comes expecting to be given at least some last-minute crumb of hope, some turn towards redemptive possibility. But that evening he refused to give it to them. He just went on with his crisply-articulated, vividly appalling catalogue of evidence.

In the absence of an amen, what was interesting that evening was the gusto of the speaker's delivery, a kind of evangelist zeal for realism. His face possessed that Jeremiah glow that one observes sometimes in a bearer of bad news; you sense that the speaker is relishing his role as the clear-eyed, unsentimental messenger. At the end of the evening he would be wined, dined, and thanked, but right now, he was the one whose regrettable duty it was to inform the audience that its good will, its confidence in the bottomless resourcefulness of human ingenuity was futile and self-deceiving. That was the mission on which he had been sent, and he had fulfilled his obligation.

Yet there was something adolescent about the performance as well; it had something of the smug assurance of a poker player holding a full hand of black aces. In his apocalyptic gusto, he had left us no way out of the corner he had painted us into.

Realism is a powerful state of mind. It gets things done, but its shadow side is fatalism, pessimism, and certainty, and when wielded like a club, as it often is, it can reduce us to a state of hopelessness. In the rhetorical construction of that evening, we had the sensation of being woken up on Sunday morning, but awakened too late to remedy our circumstances.

There was also something distinctively male about such a performance. One senses that the masculine desire to be sure, to be powerful with fact, has cut a bargain with reality, and, in exchange for certainty, has been willing to pay the price of hopelessness.

In one of her most famous essays of the early seventies, "When We Dead Awaken," Adrienne Rich identifies this tendency in cultural construction with characteristic acuity: "To the eye of a feminist," says Rich, "the work of Western male poets now writing reveals a deep fatalistic pessimism as to the possibilities of change, whether societal or personal. . . . The creative energy of patriarchy is running out fast; what remains is a self-generating energy for destruction."[1]

It is perhaps impossible to say exactly, but Rich was probably referring to certain poems like those included in Galway Kinnell's *The Book of Nightmares*, or perhaps certain poems by Philip Levine, James Wright, or Robert Bly, whose furious work of the time was obsessed with denouncing the militaristic tyranny of imperialism, the grandiosity and arrogance that seemed to be destroying the earth.

---

1. "When we dead awaken" Writing as Revision" 1971, from *Claims for Poetry*, edited Donald Hall (University of Michigan Press November 30, 1982), p. 361.

Here are a few samples of the period, selected from the final lines of poems by male poets—the place, in other words, where the desire for closure and certainty can tempt a writer to play a resounding minor chord.

Here are the last lines of James Wright's poem "Twilights":

The arbors of the city are withered.
Far off, the shopping centers empty and darken.

A red shadow of steel mills.

And this is from Wright's "Eisenhower's Visit To Franco, 1959":

Smiles glitter in Madrid.
Eisenhower has touched hands with Franco, embracing
In a glare of photographers.
Clean new bombers from America muffle their engines
And glide down now.
Their wings shine in the searchlights
Of bare fields,
In Spain.

Here's the end of Merwin's poem called "The Asians Dying":

The nights disappear like bruises but nothing is healed
The dead go away like bruises . . .
Overhead the seasons rock
They are paper bells
Calling to nothing living

The possessors move everywhere under Death their star
Like columns of smoke they advance into the shadows
Like thin flames with no light
They with no past
And fire their only future

Here are a few lines from late in Galway Kinnell's poem "The Dead Shall Be Raised Incorruptible":

A few bones
lie about in the smoke of bones.

Effigies pressed into grass,
mummy windings,
desquamations, . . .
angel's wings
flagged down into the snows of yesteryear,

kneel
on the scorched earth
in the shapes of men and animals:

do not let this last hour pass,
do not remove this last, poisoned cup from our lips. . . .

Lieutenant!
This corpse will not stop burning!

Rich saw clearly that the masculine mind—even those of our best-intentioned male poets—was fatally addicted to scenarios of destruction, revenge, and repetition. These men could not, it seems, manage to think of a new story. But the final sentence in Rich's essay strikes a stalwart and heroic note: "As women," she says, "we have our work cut out for us."

It is easy enough in our own moment to feel helpless and fatalistic. That temptation is strong. When we consider the technological and media powers we have inadvertently unleashed against ourselves, and against nature itself, when we see how these enormously magnified, gargantuan powers have been co-opted by the corporate forces of greed and hubris—even Adrienne Rich and her peers might give in to hopelessness.

One wonders—and perhaps it is superfluous even to ask—are these instincts really characteristically male? Yet, look, after all, at the faces of the American generals and executive leaders on display on TV—grim, unsmiling, bulldog faces; the rigid, inexpressive faces of old toads, warty with humorless duty, certain that they can correct the world by inflicting terrible damage upon it. In thousands of years, it seems, nothing has changed. Again and again, we still somehow sign over our fates to such faces.

Honoring the Revisionary Powers of Imagination

And so, at a time like this, it is important to turn toward the counter-powers of language and imagination, and to recall what resides there—not merely the solaces of distraction or beauty, but our active ability to rewrite reality into stories of progression, and evolution, stories that we could thrive on.

Though fantasy has often been described as an escapist impulse in literature and life, in fact it also has a corrective relationship to the god of realism; it can discover pathways that can be examined and invested in. Like free-flowing water, sometimes fantasy can find a way through and around seemingly immoveable obstructions. In a time when the inherited imagination seems brutal, unreal, and insufficient, fantasy can rise to a level more real than the facts.

Many poems by the Israeli poet Yehuda Amichai place the spirit of fantasy in dialogue with the spirit of realism. (One of the wonderful things about his poetry is that it does not foreclose on either territory.) Amichai's "An appendix to the vision of peace" is a witty, dead-serious development of the Old Testament's prophecy of peace, Isaiah's prediction that "no longer shall nation lift up sword against nation . . . they shall beat their swords into ploughshares." Here's what Amichai does with it:

Don't stop after beating the swords
into ploughshares, don't stop! Go on beating
and make musical instruments out of them.

Whoever wants to make war again
will have to turn them into ploughshares first.[2]

Amichai's poem operates by a kind of embellishment and extension of its source. If the original text implies that a plough would be a more worthy tool than a sword (the shift from a war

2. "An appendix to the vision of peace" copyright 1997 by Yehuda Amichai. Translated by Glenda Abramson and Tudor Parfitt. Reprinted from *Great Tranquility: Questions and Answers* with permission from Sheep Meadow Press. All rights reserved.)

culture to an agri-culture), then Amichai's fantasy proposes a civilization that has progressed to an even higher level—one that loves melody and song more than hard labor.

His proposal may be irrational from the perspective of "realism." This music-loving society may not come to exist in any literal sense (but why not)? Nonetheless, fantasy's work here is to be *truer* than fact, to be so vivid that it wakes us up and shows us a way through. Call it serious playfulness.

Even the *duration* of the poem's imagistic permutations may be instrumental in its magic; step by step, it guides us farther away from the seductions of aggression. The poem's methodical transformations infect the reader with a sort of patience. Amichai's poem calms and relaxes us in a way that illustrates another of the utilitarian virtues of fantasy—it tutors us in internal *elasticity*. And, as an argument, Amichai's sleights of hand are strangely more convincing than the strident, self-righteous denunciations of your typical anti-war poem. Here, fantasy becomes a peacemaker.

In her poem, "On the Occasion of Being Mistaken for a Man by the Cashier in the Drive-Thru Window at a Wendy's in Madison, Wisconsin," poet Stacey Waite also models the way that fantasy can serve as a corrective lens for reality. In Waite's poem, fantasy doesn't seem *escapist*; rather it rectifies the world and restores proportion.

> When a woman does it, I feel more like a man.
> Simone at the Wendy's drive-through makes me feel
> more like a man when she says, "Out of ten, sir?"
> and she leans her breasts atop the little shelf
> at the folding window, smiles. "You have gorgeous hands,"
> I say. I can't even see her hands, but tonight
> I have license to compliment, to tell Simone
> I have never seen more delicate hands.
>
> In a perfect world, I wouldn't tell Simone I was an
>   "anatomical female"
> until our fourth date. I would include this in the same
>   sentence
> that tells her my grandparents speak Slovak and my brother

is a restaurant owner. And Simone would sway in
and kiss my neck and say, "Really? isn't that interesting?"
And over dinner with her parents, her father
would not forget to ask me about my brother,
about whether we could all go out for a free meal.

In a perfect world, Simone's voice is a cocoon,
an agent of transformation and Simone is a drive-thru queen
who gives us all permission to stop
dividing like cells, to stop making her leave me
on our fourth date and never speak a word about me.[3]

The "perfect world" Waite's poem invokes is not a preposterous, cotton-candy or sentimental fantasy, but the projection of
a not-so-impossible, more sane, more elastic and decent place,
one in which gender is not a location of rigidity and fright. "In a
perfect world," she says, "Simone's voice is a cocoon, / an agent
of transformation and Simone is a drive-thru queen / who gives
us all permission to stop / dividing like cells."

Waite's poem is not an escapist denial of contemporary realities. In fact, the speaker is quite meticulous in her description of
the social status quo. But though the reality principle asserts itself in the poem's final two lines, Waite's detailed envisioning of
an alternative narrative makes it a plausible future, one in which
no one is overly shocked or outraged by shifting social realities.

Danez Smith's poem "dinosaurs in the hood," published in
2017, offers a powerful rewrite of the stereotypical narrative of
inner city despair. Like Waite's poem, Smith's is painstaking in
describing the status quo. But in the poem, the speaker refuses
the conventional tragic versions of urban realism, and supplants
them with a better narrative. His instrument is the stubborn and
inventive counter-power of imagination. Smith's images and
deft, dark humor make the affirmative urgent and in some mysterious, poignant way, convincing:

let's make a movie called *Dinosaurs in the Hood*.
Jurassic Park meets *Friday* meets *The Pursuit of Happyness*.

---

3. Reprinted with permission from Stacey Waite.

there should be a scene where a little black boy is playing
with a toy dinosaur on the bus, then looks out the window
& sees the *T. rex*, because there has to be a *T. rex*.

don't let Tarantino direct this. in his version, the boy plays
with a gun, the metaphor: black boys toy with their own lives
the foreshadow to his end, the spitting image of his father.
nah, the kid has a plastic brontosaurus or triceratops
& this is his proof of magic or God or Santa. i want a scene

where a cop car gets pooped on by a pterodactyl, a scene
where the corner store turns into a battle ground. . . .
this movie is about a neighborhood of royal folks—

children of slaves & immigrants & addicts & exile—saving
    their town
from real ass dinosaurs. . . .
        i want grandmas on the front porch taking out raptors

with guns they hid in walls & under mattresses. i want those
    little spitty
screamy dinosaurs. i want Cicely Tyson to make a speech,
    maybe two.
i want Viola Davis to save the city in the last scene with a
    black fist afro pick
through the last dinosaur's long, cold-blood neck. But this
    can't be
a black movie. this can't be a black movie. this movie can't
    be dismissed

because of its cast or its audience. this movie can't be a
    metaphor
for black people & extinction. This movie can't be about
    race.
this movie can't be about black pain or cause black pain.
this movie can't be about a long history of having a long
    history with hurt.
this movie can't be about race. . . .

no bullet holes in the heroes. & no one kills the black boy. &
    no one kills
the black boy. & no one kills the black boy. besides, the only
    reason

I want to make this is for that first scene anyway: little black
    boy
on the bus with a toy dinosaur, his eyes wide & endless

                his dreams possible, pulsing, & right
                there.[4]

Smith's poem acknowledges and describes the American narrative of racial fatalism, movies in which black boys must have
guns and die, in which the characters are stereotypically disenfranchised and doomed. What is atypical is the way that Smith's
speaker asserts that "this can't be a black movie" about race,
"can't be dismissed because of its cast or audience." Fantasy
wielded by an adult consciousness is often a defiant reclamation
of the rights of childhood, and this is true of Smith's poetry in
general, but "dinosaurs in the hood" has many other valences
as well. The new narrative must not just denounce the old one,
but leave it behind. His poem-film "dinosaurs in the hood" has
to be a *human* movie, a movie with humor, a movie in which a
whole surprising community of characters can do battle against
the "dinosaurs" of the past, and win. Smith insists on a narrative
in which imagination is resourceful, tough and alternative.

The shadow side of realism is often fatalistic. The authoritative
prediction of defeat and doom is the great temptation of a so-
called realist, for poets as well as for generals. To judge, to con-
demn, to lament, even to be hopeless—all forms of finality are
a temptation to us. Political poems are especially susceptible to
the temptations of absolutism. For it feels like a kind of power
to get angry and denounce, to predict the certain end of the
world. But these are not the only kind of poems we need right
now. As Amichai says, "In the place where we are right, flowers
will never grow."

But some dreams have the power to show a way through.
Such visions may be stumbled upon almost accidentally through

---

4. "dinosaurs in the hood" copyright 2017 by Danez Smith. Reprinted from
Don't Call Us Dead with permission from the author and Graywolf Press. All rights
reserved. www.graywolfpress.org

daydreaming, or extruded into existence by inner necessity. The world bank of literature and poetry is itself a kind of trust fund or legacy of our collective imagination—the treasures there can remind us of the solutions creative people have found in the past—and the future.

American social reality may have offered little "realistic" promise for the future Martin Luther King saw in his "I Have a Dream" speech, but his visionary fantasy enabled him to envision it. Life, with its tendency to grow constricted, requires new stories, and there may be times when we may only find them through the practice of fantasy. Fantasy is a reservoir, a mode of seeking, and a secret cache of hope.

Greatness Is All Around Us

I was walking down a street in New York a few years ago, with an older, wiser poet-friend who pronounced, "Philip Levine has written two great poems: "You Can Have It," and "They Feed They Lion." Though I didn't automatically agree with his selections, or their number, I admired my friend's certainty. It pleased me, and pleases me afresh to think that a great poem would definitively be recognized, confidently identified, and spoken of as such.

I grew up as a member of probably the last generation who heard other poets or scholars say things like "His poems shall be remembered as long as the English language is spoken." Then everyone in the audience would solemnly nod in agreement with what seems (now) like a preposterous grandiosity.

The last generation of poets who thought that way about themselves, in America, at least, was that of Robert Lowell, and Delmore Schwartz, and John Berryman. They had inherited a faith in the monumentality of culture, the vision that even if the world fell into nuclear ruin, great paintings and music and poetry, too, would still stand like marble statues in the desert, a testament to the ingenuity and beauty of the human mind.

And, somehow or other, they were endowed with the vanity or ambition to believe that their own poetry might stand in that elect rank.

We don't talk like that anymore, and probably it is wise that we don't, for a number of reasons, and yet I still very much care about that idea of measurable quality; the idea that a consensus can exist between serious readers about what is great and what is merely good. I have a belief that we can tell the gold from the silver, the copper from the lead.

But the transience of culture, the increased volume of info-stimulation, the disposability of culture, our ever-more-swiftly-heightened awareness of issues of cultural and gender diversity and its role in taste, calls that standard of inarguable greatness into question for many people. "There are many kinds of great," they say, "there are different greats. You like old-white-man greats. I don't like that kind of great so much." I wonder how many of my peers, my generation, now—with their nervousness about elitism and canonicity—would actually even venture to declare this poet or poem "Great?" Is "great" a category now so problematical that we dare not risk using the word?

Still, I am loyal to the idea of greatness—the idea that there are ten poems I could take into a prison cell for ten years, or keep with me on a desert island, which would indefinitely nourish and amuse and inspire me. Other poems—most poems, I would say—are as good as Eveready batteries. They function well enough to keep your flashlight working. But a great poem is a like a solar panel—it will run and produce light for a very long time.

In this essay I want to say that I am sick of the popular notion that greatness is *not* around us right now. I am certain, in fact, that *many* great poems have been written since Lowell and Bishop and Berryman, since Frost's "Mending Wall" or Thomas's "Do Not Go Gentle into That Good Night." I am certain that some poets in the recent past and present could and can and should be called great, not just for individual poems, but for their bodies of work. They should be acknowledged as great.

In an essay of 1923, "How it Strikes a Contemporary," Virginia Woolf expressed agitation over the same question; why, she wondered, do there seem to be no contemporary masterpieces? Why, she asked, are contemporary critics so unable or reluctant to proclaim them? In large part, it was the critics of her era with whom she found fault, who—unlike Matthew Arnold or S. T. Coleridge—were apparently not courageous or brash enough to recognize and proclaim great works. As usual, Woolf—who has the credibility of being a great writer herself—is interesting on the subject.

> If we make a century our test, and ask how much of the work produced in these days in England will be in existence then,

we shall have to answer not merely that we cannot agree upon the same book, but that we are more than doubtful whether such a book there is. It is an age of fragments. A few stanzas, a few pages, a chapter here and there.

Thanks to media and speed (thanks, media!) we have a hundred-thousand times as much art to deal with as Woolf did in a year. We seem as baffled as she was about how to measure it. Nonetheless, I refuse the assumption that greatness is something that belongs to another era; that one more book must be written about Robert Lowell, because he was the last identifiably, consensus-approved, board-certified heroic-scale poet in our era. I want to make the case against the timidity of academics and canon-makers, who are too insecure in their own taste to freely declare a living writer's poetry lastingly extraordinary. I equally wish to denounce the stinginess of the rest of us, who would rather not admit the definitive excellence of some work from our own generations as equal to the great work of the past.

Who are some contemporary poets whom we would nominate as great? To mention just two American examples—potentially there are many others—W. S. Merwin and Louise Glück could be easily named as poets who have written large bodies of extraordinary work that qualify them as major poets, and whose collections contain many great individual poems.

What's more, I will not say, "That's just my opinion." I believe that anyone smart, sensitive, and knowledgeable about poetry could look at twenty of the best poems by these two poets, and agree, "Yes, this is indelible and radiant work, that has lasting value and beauty, majesty and mastery of craft. These poems should and will join the permanent canon of poetry. They should be read and admired by poetry readers a hundred years from now."

What's more, I am certain that there are many, many other individual poems which are great—and many of them are by poets who are not and never will be famous, never be anointed with the Pulitzer Prize or the National Book Award. Yet these poems embody virtuosic levels of craft and powerful statements of the human condition which could easily be called great. In a *Norton Anthology* from which the names of all the authors had been redacted, these poems would stand out when encountered, and they would hold their own next to those of Larkin, or Bishop, or Eliot, or Frost.

But now I have assumed an obligation: I must produce an example of a great contemporary poem. To serve my purposes I want to offer the poem "Quarantine" by Eavan Boland.

Large in its themes, compressed in intensity, swift in development, and emotionally powerful in impact, Boland's poem, in only twenty lines, recounts a story from the Irish Famine of the mid-nineteenth century: the death by starvation of a husband and wife. "Quarantine" thus invokes the authority of history, the gravitas of tragedy, and approaches the mysteries of romantic love. In themselves, these are poetically ambitious premises. With its austere tone, it initially positions itself as a kind of objective witness to history—but the poem progressively escalates into a heroic and passionate mode:

In the worst hour of the worst season
    of the worst year of a whole people
a man set out from the workhouse with his wife.
He was walking—they were both walking—north.

She was sick with famine fever and could not keep up.
    He lifted her and put her on his back.
He walked like that west and west and north.
Until at nightfall under freezing stars they arrived.

In the morning they were both found dead.
    Of cold. Of hunger. Of the toxins of a whole history.
But her feet were held against his breastbone.
The last heat of his flesh was his last gift to her.

Let no love poem ever come to this threshold.
    There is no place here for the inexact
praise of the easy graces and sensuality of the body.
There is only time for this merciless inventory:

Their death together in the winter of 1847.
    Also what they suffered. How they lived.

154

And what there is between a man and a woman.
And in which darkness it can best be proved.

"Quarantine" is, in many ways, a quite old-fashioned poem; declarative and purposeful, it is a rhetorical vehicle which delivers a dramatic story from which it derives moral power.

One source of "Quarantine's" force is in the half-hidden internal tension between romantic and anti-romantic energies; between restraint and expressiveness, between purpose and feeling. Boland's is a didactic poem which warns against didacticism; a passionately personal poem that deceptively presents itself as chilly and tough-minded. It is also extraordinarily dynamic in its movement. In just twenty lines, its speaker's voice rises from severe objectivity to a vulnerable and passionately angry idealism, one which affirms one of the most fundamental human mysteries.

This paradoxical contradiction of anti-romantic and romantic elements is one secret of the poem's great charisma. On the one hand the speaker refuses to "heroize" the forsaken woman and man—on the other hand, she tells us that they "died of the toxins of a whole history." On the one hand, she insists this is no goddamn love poem; on the other, we are told that "The last heat of his flesh was his last gift to her." Of such deep paradox, great art is made.

The great turn in the poem occurs in its fourth, penultimate stanza, in which the speaker aims her emotional challenge towards her audience; towards the kind of facile sensibility that would in some way exploit the story of these poor human figures. That the speaker herself does no less doesn't matter. In the end perhaps, it may even be that these shadowy, partially-repressed aspects of the poem's self-knowledge—its unconscious grievances and agendas—are what lend it the charged heat of greatness. The presence of these subliminal, not entirely understood emotions redeem the poem from being merely rhetorical:

Let no love poem ever come to this threshold.
There is no place here for the inexact
praise of the easy graces and sensuality of the body.
There is only time for this merciless inventory:

These subliminal forces are especially resident in the poem's tone: the aggrieved ire of the voice of the speaker, for example, suggests a history of personal woundedness. Similarly, what we hear in "Quarantine's" general aggressiveness is the *protective* tone of a mother who is shielding her children—these small figures from history, long since dead, but still vulnerable—from the present that would exploit them into meaning. That scolding, yet honorific tone has a double effect: it marvelously chides and reduces the poem's audience, and at the same time makes us feel that we are being sheltered by a powerful adult presence.

In this brilliant poem the old standards of greatness are hardly absent or obsolete. It is firmly fixed to the tradition of great sermonic poetry, as heroic as that of Milton, Dante, or Yeats. In any case, "Quarantine" is a powerful work of art, which verifies, to me, the thesis of this essay. Read Boland's poem out loud to willing friends—perhaps more than once—and they will have an experience which verifies the fundamental importance and reason for poetry.

This essay is not meant to canonize Glück, Merwin, Boland or anyone else in particular. I merely wish to assert, with conviction, that genuinely great poetry is being made among us now. We don't need to be stingy with our praise, or unconfident in testifying to the quality, or the degree of pleasure and meaning we take from what we read now. Dozens and maybe hundreds of great poems are floating around us, poems as great in their way as anything that has been written. I believe that that we should count ourselves lucky to be among these poets and to read their poems. To confidently name them out loud to the world is not an act of charity, nor to compromise the standards of the past, but a matter of our own discriminating generosity, which does honor to others and ourselves and, most of all, to poetry itself.

Printed and bound by CPI Group (UK) Ltd, Croydon, CR0 4YY

09/06/2025

14685646-0001